Presented to:
Butler Area Public Library

In Memory of
Dean (Big Daddy) Kirk

Donor
Jackie and Norm Young

"Then **Tony** Said to **Junior.**"

The Best NASCAR Stories Ever Told

Mike Hembree

TRIUMPH
BOOKS

Library of Congress Cataloging-in-Publication Data

Hembree, Michael, 1951–
    Then Tony said to Junior— : the best NASCAR stories ever told / Mike Hembree.
        p. cm.
    Includes bibliographical references.
    ISBN 978-1-60078-090-5
    1. NASCAR (Association)—Miscellanea. 2. Stock car racing—United States—Miscellanea. I. Title.
    GV1033.H47 2008
    796.72—dc22

                                        2008042214

This book is available in quantity at special discounts for your group or organization. For further information, contact:

Triumph Books
542 South Dearborn Street
Suite 750
Chicago, Illinois 60605
(312) 939-3330
Fax (312) 663-3557

Printed in U.S.A.
ISBN: 978-1-60078-090-5
Design by Patricia Frey
All photos courtesy of Getty Images unless otherwise indicated.

*For Maggie and Gus, the best grandchildren
in the whole wide world.*

table of
contents

Chapter 12: Toil, Trouble, and No Kissing, Please 159

foreword

With the amazing coverage of every single current development and happening in NASCAR today, it's easy to dismiss some of the greatest stories of our sport because there is just too much new stuff to cover. That's too bad. There's value in those old stories, and sometimes the memories and the past experiences are more telling and more fun than the latest goings-on.

My career has been so amazing and so much fun that it's hard to explain. I'm sure you can see it in my interviews on television—I'm really enjoying this, but more and more I come to value my friends and their memories of our paths to this point.

When I get a chance to talk to guys like Rusty Wallace, Bobby Allison, and David Pearson, the coolest parts are the stories that didn't necessarily make the newspapers.

There is so much going on in this sport, and it's really a challenge. You have to understand the physics of the car. You have to manage your time well. And the competition level is really high, physically and mentally. All that is not even including all the peripheral things that go on. There is the relationship between you and your crew chief, and then you and your teammates, and you and your sponsors. You have to manage all those relationships and all those expectations. When I was 15 and 16, I hadn't even thought about the majority of that stuff. You start to understand how this whole thing works, and you start to see patterns. It's different.

I like to keep control over everything in my life when I can, but I realized early on that I had to hand some things off to other people and concentrate on the areas where I could be most productive. You have to have a lot of faith in people. It's hard. There are things where you just have to say, hey, I'm going to do the best I can and hope that that works out.

There are way too many great, great people who create so many amazing and entertaining stories to cover. This book will get into some of the best of these and give you a fun look at the people who are slowly becoming family to me—scary!

—Carl Edwards

acknowledgments

Hang around motorsports for more than a quarter-century, and several things are likely to happen. Among them, 1) You'll lose part of your hearing; 2) You'll become involved in traffic jams that are world-class in volume, intensity, and vehicle diversity; 3) You'll meet some of the most remarkable and interesting people in the world.

I can no longer hear a pin drop, and I have been in the mother of all sports-event traffic jams. And the father, the brother, and the sister.

And those remarkable people? Yes, they're around. And many of them live within the confines of press boxes and media centers across the wide sweep of NASCAR racing. With more years covering stock-car racing than I now care to tabulate, I have had the good fortune to become friends with many of the residents of these news-media encampments. I am here to report that, with the rare exception, they are some of the finest people I've run across in a varied career of chasing race cars; football, basketball, and baseball players; golfers; Olympic athletes; hurricanes; tornadoes; and the occasional criminal.

Although sports journalists tend to be as competitive as the people and teams they cover, I wouldn't hesitate to go to war—if it came to that—with the folks with whom I've shared space in media centers from one coast to the other, from cold winter Sundays in Daytona Beach to the race-day heat of Fontana, California. Contrary to what perhaps is the general perception, sportswriting is not all peaches and cream. It is much more than watching events, lining up at buffets, and hobnobbing with celebrities and athletic heroes. Those who do it best put in long hours, live out of suitcases, and deal almost daily with athletes who can be equal parts sunny and surly. Most retain the perspective that allows them to share the worlds they cover with readers who can only dream of such close contact.

Sports journalists live in a strange world. Because of their access, they move along the same roads as the athletes they cover, but they share in the victories and joys of those athletes and their fans only from the other side of a wall of separation. There is no cheering in the press box. Conversely, journalists often are much too close when tragedy strikes. They must write hard stories in hard times while striving to remain objective, and that can be one of the hardest jobs in the business.

Most of the men and women I've had the pleasure to work with over the years have navigated these sometimes choppy waters with talent, professionalism, and dedication to get the story right. The names are far too numerous to mention, but, to all, thanks for sharing the ride. It's been fun.

The stories in this book come from a wealth of sources—drivers, mechanics, team owners, public-relations representatives, officials, garage hangers-on, and assorted ne'er-do-wells who popped in and out of the sport, leaving only tall tales. Almost everyone, it seems, has a story.

Modern NASCAR racing is much more polished and proper than the sport I was introduced to in 1975 (and even then racing was like a country club in comparison to the rough-and-tough pioneer years of the sport). It isn't a real surprise that some of racing's best stories are also some of its oldest, but that might be because they somehow grow better with age.

To all those who have shared their stories over the years, here's a salute. And, for the music that helped to carry me through another book project, here's to Bruce Springsteen, John Prine, Willie Nelson, and John Hiatt. They rock, and the iPod is now high-mileage. And, to the gang on the home front—Polly, Holly, Stacey, and Chris—thanks for always being there.

chapter 1
The Man

Dale Earnhardt Sr., here relaxing on his car before the Gatorade 125-mile qualifying races on February 15, 2001, at Daytona International Speedway, is perhaps the most famous NASCAR driver of all time. Though he passed away on February 18, 2001, in a tragic accident at the Daytona 500, his legacy continues to thrive. Photo courtesy of AP Images.

It is no small salute to Dale Earnhardt Sr.
that, years after his death, his presence in
stock-car racing is very real.

It can be seen at any stop on the NASCAR Cup
tour. Thousands swing by the souvenir haulers
to buy the T-shirts, caps, and an assortment of
other paraphernalia that continues to stamp his
image on the sport. In the grandstands, fans still
stand and thrust three fingers into the sky.
Many still wear faded and battered T-shirts
from the Intimidator's glory days.

There has been no other driver quite like him.
It can be argued that some have been better,
but there is little debate that he carved a unique
spot for himself in the long timeline of the sport.

His legacy roars on.

A Tearful Day for Dale

Dale Earnhardt cultivated his image as the Intimidator, the fierce competitor who asked no quarter and gave none, the tough customer whose hard stare in your rearview mirror could produce fear and trembling.

He wasn't always that way, of course, and some drivers weren't scared of his glare, but that persona served him well on the track—and it sold a ton of T-shirts.

There was another side to the man many view as NASCAR's greatest driver ever, and it popped up in the winter of 1993.

As part of an annual racing-media tour organized by Lowe's Motor Speedway, reporters spend four days in January traveling to race shops and meeting with drivers, crew members, and other officials to preview the upcoming season. The 1993 tour included an unusual component—a chartered flight to Daytona Beach, Florida, for a day of preseason testing at Daytona International Speedway.

As a five-time champion and perennially one of the circuit's top drivers, Earnhardt was much in demand by the media. He was testing at Daytona that day, and the hundreds of reporters arriving at the speedway assumed he would be available for interviews.

They—and the tour organizers—assumed wrong.

Earnhardt refused to do one-on-one interviews or to meet with the group in a press-conference setting. Although Earnhardt was at times difficult with the news media, it was surprising for him to be so stubborn in a situation where that much time and expense had been invested to create the opportunity for so many reporters to visit with him.

The news-media contingent was outraged, and so were the tour organizers. Eddie Gossage, a friend of Earnhardt's and the speedway's public-relations director at the time, went to the speedway garage area to find Earnhardt and discuss the matter.

"He was just as mad as he could be," Gossage said. "He was poking me in the chest. He said, 'I'm not talking to you guys.

You're interrupting my work. I'm trying to win.' I got back in his face, and they wound up separating us. And he didn't talk to anybody."

The tour group went home without being enlightened by Earnhardt.

Gossage was notified later that night that his mother, Lucille Gossage, had passed away in Tennessee. He left the media tour to be with his family.

Gossage returned to work at the speedway the following Monday and found a visitor waiting in his office.

"I got in early to catch up, since I had been away," he said. "I walked down the hall and noticed that my office door was open and the light was on. I rounded the corner, and Earnhardt was sitting there. 'You sure come to work late,' he said.

"He said, 'I'm sorry about your mom.' He remembered having met her in Nashville. He said, 'Tell me about her.'

"I started talking about her, and tears came to my eyes. Then he started telling stories about his dad [the late Ralph Earnhardt], and he started crying. We talked for about 45 minutes and both had tears running down our faces.

"He said, 'I'm sorry we had a fight. I brought you a peace offering.' Then he gave me one of his helmets. He walked to the door to go, turned around and looked at me, and said, 'Don't you ever tell anybody.'"

Did Earnhardt Ride with Extra Magic?

Although superstitions aren't talked about much in modern stock-car racing, they once were items of serious consideration for many racers.

Two things that were thought to be very bad luck, for example, from the early days of racing until the 1970s, were green cars and peanuts in the pits. Perceptions of green began changing when sponsors who had green products—for example, Mountain Dew and Gatorade—wanted to sponsor teams. Suddenly, green wasn't so bad. In fact, it was downright welcome.

Some speedways also were known for unusual infield characters who, it was said, could put a "hex" on a particular driver and thus prevent that driver from doing well that day. The opposite also was true—some racetrack regulars could give a driver a boost, it was said, simply by touching his car.

This phenomenon impacted one of NASCAR's all-time greats in an unusual way. Dale Earnhardt had one of stock-car racing's all-time best résumés, with 76 Cup victories and seven national championships, but he struggled for two decades to score a victory in his sport's biggest race, the Daytona 500. He seemed to have victory locked down several times, only to have it slip away in the closing laps.

In December 1997 Earnhardt and members of the Richard Childress Racing team traveled to Greenville-Pickens Speedway (GPS) in South Carolina for two days of off-season testing. Earnhardt loved Greenville-Pickens, a half-mile track that once hosted the Cup Series. His father, Ralph, raced there many times when Dale was a child, and GPS old-timers remember a young Dale playing in the little creek that runs through the track's infield. GPS, which hasn't hosted a Cup race since 1971, remains a popular testing spot for Cup teams.

"We had a guy at the track who had told me that if he could rub that No. 3 [Earnhardt's Chevrolet], that Earnhardt would win Daytona," said track operator Tom Blackwell. "I took him over to see the car during one of their test breaks. I told him, 'Okay, you get over there and rub on that car like you said you were.' He did. Richard Childress came over and said, 'What are you doing?' He said, 'I'm going to put some magic on that car to make it win.'"

Two months later, Earnhardt finally broke through in the 500, winning the race to ignite the sort of wild celebration that is seldom seen in NASCAR racing. "The monkey is finally off my back," Earnhardt said.

A couple weeks later, Bill Elliott was at GPS testing. "Hey, where's that guy who touches cars?" he asked.

Dale Earnhardt in a Ford?

Although Dale Earnhardt won all of his seven championships and 73 of his 76 Cup victories in Chevrolets, there was a detour in his racing life. His devoted following forever links him to Chevrolet and, in particular, the black No. 3 he drove for Richard Childress Racing, but he once was a solid Ford driver. And he could have remained that.

Earnhardt raced for Bud Moore Engineering in Fords as he was trying to build the foundation for a driving career. It was his last stop before joining Childress and embarking on the wildly successful part of his career.

If the times had been different, said Moore, now retired, Earnhardt might have been a Ford driver for the rest of his career. The Blue Oval was going through tough times in its motorsports program during that period, especially with its engine performance. Ford won only two of 30 Cup races in 1982. The problems were solved later in the 1980s, but, by then, Earnhardt had sailed for clearer waters.

"I knew what type person Dale was and what type [of] driver he was beginning to be," said Moore. "We had a couple of good years. We didn't have the right parts and pieces to keep the engines together like we should. We broke a lot of valve springs and lost a lot of valves during those years. It was a tough time to be racing Fords; not because they weren't good, but because we couldn't get the pieces.

"I think that sort of discouraged Dale a little and was the reason he left me and went on to Childress."

The delicate nature of the Ford engines was in direct contrast to Earnhardt's nature—run them, and run them hard.

"I remember once at Darlington, we were leading the race and were quite a ways out front," Moore said. "I told Dale on the radio, 'Look, take it easy. Don't turn the engine so hard. We've got to watch the valve springs.' I looked at my stopwatch the next time around, and he had picked up speed. I said, 'Man, I didn't tell you to speed up. Slow down.'

"He said, 'I'm backing off now. I'm just loafing.' It was amazing. I kept after him, but it seemed like the more he loafed the faster he ran.

"The thing about Dale was, he was going to run up front. He's not going to run second. If the piece of equipment he had under him didn't take him to the front, he's going there anyway. I was sure sorry to see him leave. I knew he was going to be great."

Maybe the greatest, and Chevrolet got the benefits.

A Tough Day in No. 8

It seems almost unbelievable now, but the NASCAR Cup debut of a man who would become one of international motorsports' greatest drivers and a national sports icon passed without much significant notice.

Dale Earnhardt Sr. made his NASCAR Cup debut on May 25, 1975, in the World 600. No one could foresee at the time what an incredible impact this man would have on the sport.

Dale Earnhardt drove in a Cup race for the first time on May 25, 1975, in the World 600 (now the Coca-Cola 600) at Charlotte Motor Speedway (now Lowe's Motor Speedway). He started 33rd and finished 22nd and won $2,425, a first paycheck on the way to the multiple millions his career would produce.

There was no grand plan and no great sponsor debut behind Earnhardt's first race. He had been trying to ignite his driving career on North Carolina short tracks, having been inspired by his father, Ralph Earnhardt, one of NASCAR's best-ever short-track racers. Among those assisting Earnhardt as he banged around the regional Late Model circuit was Norman Negre, son of veteran Cup driver Ed Negre.

Earnhardt wound up hanging around Negre's modest racing shop in Concord, North Carolina. The more the younger Negre saw Earnhardt drive, the more convinced he became that Earnhardt had special talent. He went to his father with a plan.

"Norman came to me one day and said, 'Dad, Earnhardt is really a good driver,'" Ed Negre said. "He got me to listen to him. I said, 'What are you trying to tell me, that I should put him in one of my cars?' He said, 'I bet he could drive one.' I said, 'We can't hardly afford to run one car, let alone two.' So I got one car ready [for the 600] and told him, 'If you want to run him in the other car, that's your deal and his. You go down there and get it ready to race.'"

The car was a sleek Dodge Charger. It carried the No. 8, which also was Ralph Earnhardt's number (and, much later, would be Dale Earnhardt Jr.'s number).

With Norman Negre leading the crew, Earnhardt qualified the car and faced what must have seemed like an insurmountable challenge—a 600-mile race.

"He came in the pits when I didn't expect it," Ed Negre said. "I asked Norman what was wrong. He said, 'There's nothing wrong.' He laughed and said Dale stopped for a drink of water. He'd never run a 600-mile race. He was one worn-out kid when that race was over."

Earnhardt finished 45 laps off the pace of race winner Richard Petty, who, ironically, shares the Cup record for national championships with Earnhardt at seven.

"I didn't realize at that time what my part in racing was or where I was going," Earnhardt said later. "I just wanted to race, and I had the opportunity to drive Ed's car. Ed did that himself. He didn't have a sponsor or anybody to buy tires. As a matter of fact, I think we ran used tires all day that we got from other people."

Unfortunately, Negre didn't keep the car Earnhardt raced that day. His brief tie-in with the future champion did pay off, however. "They made a die-cast model of the car later on, and I made more money off those cars than I did while I was racing," he said.

It's also worth noting that, in his debut, Earnhardt finished one position in front of Richard Childress, the man he would later join to make motorsports history. That's an odd circumstance that came up in Earnhardt-Childress conversations on more than one occasion over the years.

Did Earnhardt Plan to Quit?

Before Dale Earnhardt was killed on the last lap of the 2001 Daytona 500, he had made no public pronouncements about his racing future. He wanted to win an eighth Cup championship and break the record-tie he shared with Richard Petty, but he had given no public indication that he would retire in one, two, or even five years.

Some close friends had urged Earnhardt to quit driving. He had built a successful Cup team, had won everything in sight, had invested his millions wisely, and could easily afford to detour onto easy street.

There certainly was nothing else to prove, as friends repeatedly reminded him, but Earnhardt loved driving and the give-and-take of the competition.

"Race day is a fun day; that's what keeps me going," he said in August 2000, six months before his death. "The bottom line is that I'm excited about driving a race car. I still want to win. When I get in behind that steering wheel, I'm not happy with where I'm at unless I'm close to the front or in the front. That has kept me going.

"There are some that want to write me off. Somebody has a tough streak, and somebody writes that he needs to get out of it. That happens, but I've always felt confident that we could do it, that I could do it."

Many believe, however, that if Earnhardt had won his eighth championship in 2001 that he would have parked his race cars for good.

It's Dale Earnhardt Ink

Scott Tappan will carry his allegiance to seven-time Cup champion Dale Earnhardt with him forever.

That's because it's there in ink in a huge tattoo across Tappan's right shoulder blade.

More than a few fans show support for their favorite drivers by having car numbers or sponsors tattooed on various parts of their bodies, but few have gone to Tappan's extreme. His huge tattoo includes Earnhardt's face and his black No. 3 race car.

An industrial electrician from Sayre, Pennsylvania, Tappan got the tattoo the week after Earnhardt was killed in the 2001 Daytona 500.

In two sessions totaling 10 hours, a nearby tattoo artist put Earnhardt and his race car on Tappan's upper right back.

When Tappan takes off his shirt at races, fans want to take photographs of the tattoo, he said.

Asked why he put the Earnhardt Sr. tattoo on the right side of his back, Tappan said, "Junior. He's going on the other side."

Martin vs. Earnhardt

Dale Earnhardt was a racer's racer, a man respected by virtually everybody who drove against him. New drivers didn't automatically get respect from Earnhardt. They had to earn it.

Mark Martin has built a reputation similar to Earnhardt's in that Martin is among the most respected drivers among his peers in the sport's history. To get to that point, Martin had to have his "moment" with Earnhardt, who always put newcomers to the test.

"Dale Earnhardt tested me for fun," Martin said. "It was entertainment for Dale. He wanted to see what I would do, because Dale was that kind of guy. I took it for just a little bit, and then I had to stand up to him, but I did it differently than Geoff Bodine [who had a famous series of on-track confrontations with Earnhardt] did. Sparks flew every time those guys got within a quarter of a mile of each other; whereas I handled my deal with Dale differently, and nobody really noticed, except maybe the crews.

"I earned his respect, and we went on, but there was a period of time when he wanted to see what I was made of and how I would react, and I guess I reacted in a way that he could respect and some others didn't. The ones that didn't, he just continually kept on, and sparks flew."

Martin and Earnhardt never had a significant problem after Martin stood his ground—however quietly.

Earnhardt: It's All Competition

Dale Earnhardt was one of the most competitive racers in the history of NASCAR. He'd race you hard for first place or 20th place, particularly in the last laps, when it came time to pay money and pay points.

That part of the sport—the intense, close-quarters fighting for positions in the heat of the moment—kept Earnhardt's blood pumping and made him one of the toughest drivers to pass.

The competition drove him. In an interview in 2000, several months before he died, he talked about it.

"You go back to the start of time," he said. "One cave guy was fighting another cave guy because his club was bigger than his or his woman had longer hair. That's competition. It's been that way from the start of time. Or those apples are redder on that tree over there. Let's go over there. We're racing, and it's competition."

Bristol Matches Old Friends

Bristol Motor Speedway's annual night race, held in late summer, is a phenomenon. Fireworks aren't just expected; they're virtually assured. Before a full house of more than 160,000 fans on a hot August night on a tight racetrack, weird stuff goes on. In several fan surveys, the race has been voted the best on the schedule, and tickets are difficult to come by.

Part of the track's dramatic summer-race history was written on August 28, 1999, when Dale Earnhardt scored one of his most controversial victories. Never one to be shy, Earnhardt booted leader Terry Labonte between the first and second turns on the last lap, sending Labonte into a spin. Earnhardt slipped by on the inside and won the race as Labonte's car caused a multicar wreck behind him.

Earnhardt's roughhousing upset Labonte, although Earnhardt said his intention was only to "rattle his cage." A week later, with the circuit having moved on to Darlington, South Carolina, Labonte talked about the dramatic finish of the Bristol race.

"Believe me, if Dale had to do it over again, he wouldn't have done it," said Labonte of his longtime friend and hunting buddy. "I know that. He's a seven-time champion. The guy has a tremendous amount of talent. I'm sure he regrets that he did that. I'm not going to hold it against him. We still lost the race, and we're still disappointed that we lost the race.

"If you're trying to race somebody for the win, and you get into them, hey, you get into them. That's the way it goes. If that happens, you can't do anything about it. To me, that's racing. When you deliberately run into the back of them and turn them around, then I think that goes over the line. That's a little bit different, and I think that should be handled differently."

Officials let the order of the Bristol finish stand. Videotape of the wreck didn't prove that Earnhardt intentionally caused Labonte to crash, they said.

Labonte said he didn't plan any retaliatory moves, and there was no evidence over the next few races that he had anything like that in mind.

"It's over. It's done," he said. "Forget about it. That's all you can do. Nobody hates it happened any worse than I do, except maybe Dale. I know if he had to do it over again, it wouldn't have happened. It did, and we can't let that have any long-term effects. I've never held a grudge against anybody. I'm not going to hold one against him. I know if it comes down to the last lap somewhere, I might treat him a little bit different than I would somebody else.

"I've known him for a long time, and he's known me for a long time. We've raced together for several years. I hate it happened, and I know he hates it happened. You've just got to go on."

As Earnhardt traveled from victory lane to the postrace winner's interview in the press box late on that Bristol evening, a huge crowd formed around the elevator door he walked through. The boisterous throng seemed to be evenly divided in support of and opposition to Earnhardt's winning move. As the elevator door closed, most of them were yelling at him—some for, some against.

Smiling after the door closed, Earnhardt said, "God, I love this shit."

At Darlington, Earnhardt expressed regret at how the Bristol race concluded.

"I hate it happened with Terry and I like it did," he said. "I have a lot of respect for Terry. We've gotten along good all the years we've raced together. There's no need to get in that kind of situation with him. I haven't talked to him yet. He's been busy, and I've been busy. I don't want to make a big deal about it with everybody around. He said on ESPN he was going to shoot my horse out from under me the next time we went hunting. The last time we went hunting, I carried his gun for him, so I'll have to give him his gun to do that."

Oddly enough, Earnhardt and Labonte had been involved in another big late-race crash at Bristol four years earlier.

In that event, Labonte had the lead going into the final turn. Earnhardt, in second, pushed into the rear of Labonte's car as they left the turn, but Labonte retained control long enough to cross the finish line first, despite hitting the wall.

On that night, Labonte had the gun.

A Father's Influence

In an era in which it seems that every successful race-car driver started turning left a few months after he climbed out of the crib, it's somewhat surprising to look back and realize that one of the sport's all-time greats was 20 years old when he took his first green flag.

Dale Earnhardt raced for the first time at the age of 20 when a friend needed a driver for a jalopy race. Dale had watched his father, Ralph, race for many years and was more than ready to give it a try.

"I don't know where I finished, but it didn't really matter, since the exhilaration I got was what I remember," Earnhardt said in an interview in 1980.

Ralph Earnhardt, who died of a heart attack in 1973, was one of the best short-track racers in NASCAR history. As a kid, Dale watched him work on race cars in his backyard shop in Kannapolis,

Ralph Earnhardt was one of the best short-track racers in NASCAR history. He started a legacy that has become one of the most powerful forces in NASCAR.

North Carolina. Dale's first "seat time" in a racer came at that location when his father let the youngster drive his car in the driveway.

"The sensation was just unreal," Dale said. "I knew then that driving a race car was what I had to do."

On numerous occasions, including after he won his seventh championship in 1994, Earnhardt talked about the influence of his father.

"He is why I'm here," Earnhardt said. "My dad was the focus of my life. I didn't like school. I wanted to be home working on Dad's race car. I wanted to be home working on cleaning up the shop. I didn't like school. I'd just as soon be washing wrenches.

"He'd race on Thursday night in Columbia, South Carolina, and he'd get back in about four or five in the morning. I'd get up early, and before I'd go to school I'd go around and look at the race car. I could just about tell you what kind of night he had. If there was a whole lot of dirt and stuff on the front of it, he ran second or third to somebody. If there was very little on the front, he probably won the race or ran second."

Horse Spins Out

Driver Dale Earnhardt and team owner Richard Childress formed one of the most formidable partnerships in NASCAR history. They won six championships together and were near-permanent residents of victory lane throughout their time together.

But the Earnhardt-Childress relationship went much deeper. They were best friends, hunting and fishing buddies, and compadres of the first order.

Childress, who has hunted big game all over the world, often accompanied Earnhardt on hunting trips, particularly in the West. One such trip—to New Mexico in 1994—resulted in what Earnhardt described as a wreck.

"The mountain is so steep, you have to get off and lead your horses," Earnhardt said of the terrain. "Things were going along pretty good. It was about 7:30 in the morning, and we wanted to be up there about daylight. We had several hundred more feet to go. The way we were having to climb, we figured it would take about another half an hour. We were leading the horses, and they were lunging up on rocks, climbing around. I'm following the guide, and my horse slips. His rear feet slip off the rock, and he starts slipping. Richard is directly behind my horse. My horse goes down the left side on my gun, and I've got hold of a pine tree, and I've got hold of the reins.... When I released the reins, I realized Richard was behind the horse. As a matter of fact, he was about under the horse at that point.

"The next time I see Richard, he's diving straight down. He's tumbling, and the horse is falling about 50 feet down the mountain. They hit pine trees at just about the same time. The horse was standing up when he hit the pine tree, and Richard was in one backward. I'm looking down, and the other outfitter is going down the mountain, and Richard's got blood on his face. He was saying, 'I'm okay.'

"It wasn't funny. Blood was really flying. I thought he had broken his nose. The horse was okay, and Richard was okay, but he's got a couple of scratches on him. It was a heck of a wreck."

Earnhardt Wrote a Long History

Dale Earnhardt's racing career was filled with success and accomplishment, and much of that history was relived by his fans and the media after Earnhardt's death on the last lap of the Daytona 500 in 2001.

Although it's difficult to rank moments in Earnhardt's career, during which he captured seven national championships and a fortune in winnings, here are 10 that stand out:

April 1, 1979: Earnhardt scores his first career win, at Bristol Motor Speedway.

May 17, 1987: Earnhardt outguns Bill Elliott in a fierce race in the Winston all-star event at Charlotte Motor Speedway. The event became famous for the so-called "pass in the grass," although there actually was no pass. Earnhardt was bumped onto the grass but maintained his speed and kept the lead.

October 23, 1994: Earnhardt clinches his seventh Cup championship, at North Carolina Speedway in Rockingham.

August 5, 1995: Earnhardt wins the second Brickyard 400.

August 1996: Earnhardt sets track-qualifying record and leads 51 of first 54 laps at the Watkins Glen, New York, road course despite driving with a broken sternum and collarbone suffered in a crash two weeks earlier.

February 16, 1997: Earnhardt finishes the Daytona 500, despite the fact that his car had barrel-rolled on the backstretch and sustained heavy damage.

February 15, 1998: Earnhardt finally wins the Daytona 500 after 19 misses.

June 11, 1999: Earnhardt outruns son Dale Jr. in the final turn of the final lap to win an International Race of Champions event at Michigan International Speedway.

August 28, 1999: At Bristol Motor Speedway, Earnhardt races to win by bumping leader Terry Labonte from first place on the last lap.

October 15, 2000: Earnhardt drove an almost magical race at Talladega, Alabama, moving from 18th place to first in the closing laps to score his final career win.

Edging into the Night

Although nighttime superspeedway racing has been a big hit in NASCAR racing for more than a decade, it didn't meet with immediate approval from all parties involved when Lowe's Motor Speedway tried it for the first time for the Winston All-Star Race in 1992.

Among those who initially questioned the concept was none other than seven-time champion Dale Earnhardt, who said he was a little concerned about vision on the track and glare from the lights.

"Racing's got a safety factor," he said. "I've never worried too much about it, and I'm still not worried as far as getting hurt. I don't want to lose, and I don't want to get into a wreck unnecessarily. "I have problems on a bright, sunny day sometimes seeing oil or debris on the track. There'll be more shadows than you ever thought about. Running 170 miles per hour at Charlotte is going to be pretty exciting if you run over a piece of debris or into some oil."

But Earnhardt didn't back down from the challenge.

"I'll be there racing wide-open, whether I can see a damn thing or not," he said.

Earnhardt Almost Gave It Up

Only a few years before he won his first NASCAR Cup championship, Dale Earnhardt almost gave up on his big-time racing dreams.

He was running Sportsman races and having success and was trying his hand at superspeedway racing, but he was in the middle of a huge financial struggle, hoping to make racing work while also grinding to produce enough dollars to survive.

He was $11,000 in debt and was giving serious thought to quitting his superspeedway efforts.

"That probably would have been a disaster," he said later. "If you're serious about racing, you don't cut back—ever. You can't run a few races here and there and miss a few here and there. When you do that, you fall out of the picture. People don't see you around every week, and they forget about you.

"You've got to be there if they come looking for you."

Earnhardt was right. In October 1978 he was offered a temporary ride in a Sportsman car owned by California businessman Rod Osterlund. Within a few weeks, Earnhardt had moved into Osterlund's Cup cars, and he drove them to the Rookie of the Year title in 1979 and to the national championship in 1980.

Less than three years after considering a move away from the sport, Earnhardt was on his way to stardom and riches. He had gone from $11,000 in debt to an eight-room house on Lake Norman near Charlotte, a speedboat, a two-level boathouse, and the admiration of millions.

Dale's Last Run to Glory

Dale Earnhardt's last Cup victory was also one of his most dramatic.

On October 15, 2000, Earnhardt, using the knowledge and skills built from decades of racing at NASCAR's biggest track, played the draft perfectly and advanced from 18th place to first over the final five laps to finish in front of Kenny Wallace and Joe Nemechek.

For days and weeks after the race, observers were trying to figure out how Earnhardt was able to click off so many positions in such a relatively short span of time. The remarkable characteristics of the race became even more special the following February when Earnhardt was killed at Daytona, and the Talladega victory became his last.

Of all the perspectives of the final laps of the race, Dale Earnhardt Jr. had one of the best. He finished 14th in the wild, draft-packed rush to the checkered flag.

Later, Junior would call that race his best memory of his father's experiences at Talladega.

"Being in that race and being right—I was running second, thinking I was in a position to try to get me a win, and I can see him and his line form on the outside coming up, getting closer and closer," Junior said. "Every time I look in the mirror, he'd moved up a few more feet toward us and was coming on. So everybody was sort of in a panic mode. Everybody on the bottom line was sort of in panic mode as to—wait a minute, now, this thing ain't playing out like we had in mind.

"That was pretty cool. That was fun, because he was really proud that he was…he sort of had a way of, you know, doing all kinds of stuff like that, making big comebacks or big, great saves

In mid-October, before what would be Dale Earnhardt Sr.'s last Cup victory, father and son share a moment watching cars practice at Talladega.

or just crazy passes. And everybody always said he could do a lot of things with a race car that a lot of other people couldn't. He'd take pride in those things personally. He never would get out and jump up and down and brag about it. But, you know, when it was all said and done and over with, everybody went home, and he would take pride in doing those things.

"I think that comeback was one he really, really enjoyed."

The Bride Wore Black

Chris and Tina Dieringer of Canton, Ohio, think of themselves as the ultimate Dale Earnhardt fans.

And there's plenty of evidence to support that theory.

On April 29 (Earnhardt's birthday) of 2004, Chris and Tina were married in front of the statue of Earnhardt in Kannapolis, North Carolina, the driver's hometown.

Tina wore black for her wedding—an Earnhardt T-shirt.

"I just bawled," she said. "I kind of looked behind me, and there was Earnhardt. Just knowing he was there and part of [the wedding] made me cry."

On January 28, 2006, the Dieringers welcomed the first baby to their family. They named her Daytona Rose Dieringer—Daytona because of Earnhardt's many successes at Daytona International Speedway and his eternal connection to the track.

Among Daytona Rose's first gifts? A very, very small Earnhardt jacket.

Pilgrim Gets His Ride

One of the last races Dale Earnhardt participated in before he was killed in the Daytona 500 in 2001 was the 24 Hours of Daytona, also held at Daytona International Speedway.

The race was special for Earnhardt, largely because he raced on a team with his son, Dale Jr. Also on the Chevrolet Corvette team were road racers Andy Pilgrim and Kelly Collins. The team finished fourth.

During practice for the 24 Hours, Earnhardt Sr. and Pilgrim developed a close relationship. Pilgrim was key in teaching the two Earnhardts how to get the fastest speeds on the Daytona road course.

After the race, Earnhardt Sr. said he would try to work out a deal to give Pilgrim a ride in one of his NASCAR cars.

Shortly thereafter, Earnhardt was killed in the Daytona 500, and the talk about Pilgrim racing in NASCAR was largely forgotten. There was an exception, however.

Earnhardt Jr. remembered the conversation and gave Pilgrim the opportunity to race in a NASCAR event six years later when the Busch Series visited Montreal.

Pilgrim drove one of Junior's Busch cars to a 15th-place finish in the 203-mile race over the Circuit Gilles Villeneuve course, and a good deed Earnhardt Sr. had planned several years before was fulfilled.

chapter 2
A Rising Son

Dale Sr. and Dale Jr. shared a very close bond, which can be seen here before a race in Daytona Beach on February 4, 2001. Junior has done much to propel the Earnhardt legacy that he inherited from his father.

Simply because of his name, Dale Earnhardt Jr.'s life has been both charmed and cloaked in shadows.

To be the son of the driver many consider NASCAR's best-ever is to be both the prime carrier of a legacy and the centerpiece of expectation. He has said many times that he is not his father and that he can't compete with his father's accomplishments, but still there are the expectations.

He is like his father in many ways but also has navigated the waters of fame and fortune to build his own image and style.

Dale Jr.: Standard-Bearer, or Not?

Is Dale Earnhardt Jr. the driving force behind NASCAR's momentum?

Many observers would say yes. Earnhardt Jr.'s souvenir sales are far ahead of the second-place driver's—usually Jeff Gordon—and Junior T-shirts and caps are the most readily evident at most tracks. His trailers in the souvenir villages generally draw the biggest crowds.

Although Earnhardt clearly understands his place in the sport and the fact that he wields more economic power than many of his peers, he shies away from absorbing too much credit.

"The sport is going where it's going without Dale Earnhardt Jr.," he said. "I don't think I'm the lead locomotive here and never have. There are a lot of drivers and personalities that make up the sport. What powers the sport and fuels the sport are the media, the press, the networks, the coverage, and all the free advertisement we get from racing every weekend.

"People are tuning in and latching on to the sport for the first time. That's going to happen no matter who is driving in the sport. I feel pretty fortunate that I came along when I did. I'd have liked to have been around back in the '70s and to have known what it was like to race back then when it was a lot simpler, but the way the sport is now and how exciting it is, it's really awesome to be a part of it at this time, too."

Junior: Pearson Would Be Fun

NASCAR fans love to see showdowns at "high noon" between the best drivers in the sport.

Final-lap battles between Richard Petty and David Pearson, the sport's two winningest drivers, were legendary. They finished one-two 63 times, with Pearson claiming 33 of those wins.

Battles between Bobby Allison and Petty also were barnburners, and any last-lap challenges involving names such as Cale

Yarborough, Darrell Waltrip, Dale Earnhardt Sr., Davey Allison, Tim Flock, Curtis Turner, Junior Johnson, and Fireball Roberts were sure to draw rapt attention.

Dale Earnhardt Jr., a serious student of the history of the sport, commented on which drivers he would like to face-off against in a pressure-packed, end-of-race situation.

"From a different era, it would probably be David Pearson," he said. "That's kind of tough. There was a whole group of guys. I would definitely have liked to race with Cale Yarborough. I never got to even imagine what it would be like to race against him. He was pretty tough. I liked his style."

Yarborough, who won 83 Cup races and three championships and is in several racing Halls of Fame, was well known for his last-lap skills when the heat was on. It wasn't smart to bet against him in those situations.

Junior Learns Some Lessons

Dale Earnhardt Jr. has a busy life, with a race almost every week, appearances on off-days, and details to catch up on during infrequent downtime.

He has time to watch television occasionally, though, and says he's learned a few things by following some of his favorite music channels.

"I watch a lot of VH1," Earnhardt said. "You watch those rock-and-rollers and how they go to the top and then to the bottom. They get messed up on drugs and stuff like that. It'll teach you something."

Bristol Big for Junior

Dale Earnhardt Jr. will readily admit that he favors NASCAR's "old-line" speedways, tracks like Lowe's Motor Speedway, Atlanta Motor Speedway, Daytona International Speedway, and Bristol

Dale Earnhardt Jr. celebrates after winning the NASCAR Nextel Cup Series Sharpie 500 at Bristol Motor Speedway on August 24, 2004.

Motor Speedway (BMS). All have seen changes over the years, but they remain bedrock parts of Cup racing and have long histories of competition.

Bristol is one of Earnhardt's favorites, in large part because his father, Dale Earnhardt Sr., scored his first Cup victory at the half-mile, high-banked track on April 1, 1979. When he began his Cup career, Earnhardt Jr. targeted Bristol as one of the first places he wanted to achieve success.

That goal was reached in a big way in August 2004 when Earnhardt Jr. swept the Busch and Cup races at BMS in a weekend he won't soon forget.

Earnhardt Jr. said he watched his father spin out in a race at Bristol in the mid-1980s.

"Daddy spun out on the front straightaway, and all his tires were flat, and he got lapped," Earnhardt Jr. said. "It just drove me to tears because it's such a hard track, and he was so fast, and it's a hard race to win. I came here year after year after year wanting to get to victory lane at Bristol as a kid, because it was a track he won his first race at. He had such dominant cars so many times, and something would happen, or I'd be at school and not be here when he did win.

"It's just an awesome track. When you've won a race, you feel like you've successfully navigated a minefield. It's half elation and excitement, and the other half is relief. To have swept that weekend was just amazing to me."

Junior and the Tunes

Dale Earnhardt Jr. certainly has the lead in at least one statistical category: most appearances by a NASCAR driver in music videos.

Earnhardt recorded his eighth video appearance in 2007 when he made a cameo in the music video for "Rockstar," a song by the rock group Nickelback.

Junior also has been seen in videos with the Matthew Good Band, Three Doors Down, Staind, Sheryl Crow, Trace Adkins, Jay-Z, and O.A.R.

Although his music time is limited, Earnhardt also has been known to sit in on drums when some of his friends play gigs.

Are the Spirits Riding Along?

Virtually from its first year of operation—1969—Talladega Superspeedway in Alabama has been a track of mystery.

Numerous legends have surfaced about the speedway area over the years, particularly after it was cloaked in controversy in the beginning. The inaugural race—held at the track on September 14, 1969—created some of the most riveting drama in NASCAR's history, although virtually all of it occurred off the track. Most of NASCAR's leading drivers boycotted the race after tires failed repeatedly in practice under the high speeds produced by the new track, the biggest oval in stock-car racing at 2.66 miles.

Bill France Sr., then the president of NASCAR and builder of the new speedway, declared that the event would be held despite the boycott, and he cobbled together a field of 13 Cup cars and 23 Grand Touring entries. The race, conducted at slower-than-expected speeds with judicious use of caution flags, was won by Richard Brickhouse, a virtual unknown from Rocky Point, North Carolina.

Tire technology eventually caught up with the demands of the new track, and the first-race controversy soon faded into the background. But that would not be the end of Talladega's zaniness. Cars flew out of the track during accidents. People died after bizarre accidents in the infield. Driver Bobby Isaac pulled off the track during a race and said he had heard voices tell him to quit driving, and he did just that. Tornadoes threatened to spin the whole complex into oblivion.

Rumors spread in the track's early years that it was operating under a curse because it was built on old Native American hunting grounds. This idea was debunked by area historians.

When Dale Earnhardt Jr. started racing at Talladega, he had heard all of the stories. He also knew that his father, Dale Sr., was one of the track's masters. It took only a few runs for Junior to figure out the nuances of the monster oval, and he soon was racking up wins at the track with regularity.

Still, Junior said the track had his respect, if for no other reason than its zany history.

"When I was racing Late Models in the mid-'90s, I heard the story that Bobby Isaac heard voices," Earnhardt said. "Leading the field, come in and parked it with 10 to go or whatever when he was driving Bud Moore's car. You know, I believe it. I believe if Bobby Isaac comes in with the lead with 10 to go and tells you he heard voices, you better believe it.

"I definitely have a lot of respect for the racetrack. If what they say is true, you know, it would be kind of freaky. I heard that story a long time ago, and I heard that the airport beside the track was built on an ancient Indian burial ground. I don't know if that's true or not, but that would be quite a twist. I don't know why they haven't used that in their advertisement.

"Maybe the spirits like me."

chapter 3

Horsepower and Hijinks

After Donnie Allison and Cale Yarborough crashed on the final lap of the 1979 Daytona 500, Donnie, his brother, Bobby, and Yarborough (center, in white firesuit) got into a widely televised fistfight on the track.

The NASCAR circuit is a long, complex, and busy one that stretches from coast to coast and puts thousands of racing people on the road for 10 months of the year.

NASCAR garage areas become small villages where friendships are formed, partnerships are solidified, and fishing buddies are recruited. Occasionally, poker is played.

Just as in any other community, there are comedians and jokers and those who keep the times light. The high visibility of modern stock-car racing somewhat limits the often wild and wacky shenanigans of the sport's earlier years, but some of racing's better times still can be found in occasional lunacy.

Sure, I Can Fix That

Here's a question that comes up periodically: do NASCAR mechanics change the oil in their own cars?

The answer, generally, is no. The demands of the NASCAR schedule, the longest in all of professional sports, leave little time for such standard activities on the schedules of some of the hardest-working people in sports. And most of them make enough money these days to afford the corner quickie-change.

It's safe to say, though, that the average NASCAR garage mechanic knows quite a bit more about the ins and outs of the standard road vehicle than the guy down the street. If there's a weird knocking or pinging under the hood of the family sedan, a NASCAR mechanic probably can locate the problem faster than your friendly neighborhood wrench.

It doesn't always pay to get smart racing guys to service your vehicle, however.

This was illustrated rather abruptly quite a few years ago in an infield parking area at Darlington Raceway. Bud Moore, now retired from a lifetime of racing in roles as a crew chief and team owner, was stopped by a friend as he was leaving the speedway garage area during race-week activities. "I've got a problem," the friend said. "My engine is making all kinds of noise. It sounds like the fan belt is flopping against something when I crank it. Can you stop it?"

"I'll take a look at it," Moore said. He opened the hood and located the fan belt in question. Moore reached for one of his best tools—his pocketknife—and neatly sliced the fan belt. Naturally, the noise ceased.

"There, it won't do it anymore," Moore said, and walked away.

Some Extra Fun on a Saturday Night

The history of stock-car racing is full of tales from the heyday of the Saturday-night short tracks—typically half-mile dirt speedways that held weekly programs and often served as a launching pad for drivers who became national stars.

Some of these tracks had reputations for certain levels of what might be called ancillary activity—that is, extracurricular moments that might match driver versus driver, driver versus fans, officials versus drivers, or fans versus fans. More than a few disagreements were settled by fisticuffs behind the grandstands or in the pits before the long arm of the law—if indeed there was any—stepped in to settle tempers.

Greenville-Pickens Speedway in northwest South Carolina is one of the bedrock facilities of NASCAR-style stock-car racing. Opened in 1940 as a half-mile dirt track (it was paved in 1970), GPS hosted NASCAR's Cup Series from 1951 through 1971 and remains a strong force in weekly racing.

The track once had a reputation for fierce racing and occasional "personal interaction." Drivers visiting GPS from out of the area often became villains to the track's regular fans, and longtime short-track racer "Little" Bud Moore, who traveled from the Carolina coast to race the locals, fell into that category.

"Greenville-Pickens? Oh, yeah," Moore said. "You could get cut up there. Even by the men.

"Another thing about Greenville-Pickens was that there were a few of us—me, Tiny [Lund], LeeRoy [Yarbrough], guys like that— who ran at a lot of tracks and would go in there and race against the locals. That didn't work if it was just one of us. You didn't have a chance, because they'd all gang up on you. But if Tiny or LeeRoy was there, it was different. You had a chance."

Still, as Moore and others remember it, you sometimes had to defend your winnings with your fists, and an occasional disturbed fan might follow you out of town in his pickup.

If You Can't Beat 'Em, Beat the Car

Joe Frasson is an interesting character who bounced around the edges of stock-car racing for many years. He ran short tracks and

Cup races and had modest success here and there, although he never took the checkered flag first at the Cup level.

Frasson is perhaps best-remembered for being an oddball and creating comic relief in a garage area that, over the years, became all too businesslike.

This was never more evident than in May 1975, when Frasson brought a Pontiac Grand Prix to Charlotte Motor Speedway to attempt to qualify for the World 600, NASCAR's longest race.

The week did not go well. While all the talk at the track was about star driver Richard Petty and his quest to end a long winless streak on the one-and-a-half-mile course, Frasson struggled to get his car up to speed. It was a quest for fire that didn't work. He failed to qualify for the 40-car field.

A few minutes after the final round of time trials ended, Frasson, quite disturbed by his failure to make the race, attracted a small crowd in the garage area by—of all things—attacking his race car. Literally.

While amused mechanics watched, Frasson bashed the hood of his car with a jack handle, crumpling it.

"I want to publicly announce the retirement of the Pontiac," he said.

NASCAR was not amused. Frasson was fined $100 and suspended from competition for 15 days.

The Pontiac? It wasn't seen for a while.

A Place for Kenseth's Trophies

As their careers accelerate, NASCAR drivers tend to want the biggest and best of everything—from street cars to motorcycles to motor homes to houses.

Some are notoriously guarded with their paychecks, however. Mark Martin once said his then-teammate, Carl Edwards, was "so tight he wouldn't even get cable TV."

And Matt Kenseth, another teammate of Martin's at Roush Fenway Racing, also has a reputation for remaining pretty close to his dollars. Kenseth and his wife, Katie, built a new house near Mooresville, North Carolina, in 2006, which prompted commentary from their friend and fellow driver Ryan Newman.

"Yeah, I know Matt's got a big, new house," Newman said. "But he's so cheap all he has in it are two trophies. And one of them is his wife."

Hey, Wanna Fight?

Some of the liveliest competition in NASCAR's six-decade history has occurred away from the racing surface.

Disagreements of one sort or another occasionally spark confrontations that can lead to yelling, screaming, pushing, shoving, fighting, and name-calling—and that's just in the grandstands. Drivers and those around them sometimes get in the picture, too.

Here are three of the most noteworthy:

- On the final lap of the 1979 Daytona 500, Donnie Allison and Cale Yarborough crashed in the third turn while racing for the lead. Their crippled cars spiraled off the track and banked onto the apron. As Richard Petty inherited the race win, Allison and Yarborough got into an argument. Bobby Allison, who had stopped his car nearby to check on his brother, confronted Yarborough, which sparked a brief fight that was televised nationally.

- In August 1961, at tiny Asheville-Weaverville Speedway in the mountains of North Carolina, a Cup race ended far short of the advertised distance of 500 laps when the track's asphalt broke up. Irritated fans formed a mass of humanity across the track's exit and wouldn't let drivers and crew members leave. The standoff lasted for hours. Pop Eargle, a crew member for team owner Bud Moore, finally broke things up when he grabbed a wooden board and waded into the crowd while swinging it.

- At a 1950s-era race in Greensboro, North Carolina, drivers Tiny Lund and Lee Petty became involved in a barnburner of a fight after a disagreement. Petty's sons, Richard and Maurice, eventually joined the fray, but the Pettys weren't able to subdue Lund, a big man, until Elizabeth Petty, Lee's wife, cleared the area by swinging her pocketbook.

Kenseth Watched by "Pit Police"

Katie Kenseth, wife of Cup driver Matt Kenseth, keeps extensive notes at each race as she sits atop the Roush Fenway Racing team's pit wagon.

It's a job she learned from the very bottom level.

Katie had absolutely no experience in or around racing when she met her future husband. Now she is one of the garage's most visible and active drivers' wives.

"Katie has gotten pretty smart about the racing over the years," Matt said. "She didn't know anything at all about it when we met. From sitting on the pit box and watching and listening, she's gotten pretty smart. She talks to me a lot about the race and what went on. She scans the radios a lot to see what other people have been talking about. She gives me a lot of insight. I talk to her on the way home and learn a lot about what happened."

Crew chief Robbie Reiser noticed and gave Katie the unofficial badge of the "pit police."

"Robbie teases me and calls me that," Katie said. "Something would happen during a pit stop or on the track and, after the race, Matt would say, 'What happened?' As he would ask me more, I'd stay paying attention more. It kind of put me on the spot to pay more attention. I don't really know a lot about everything, but I know enough to be able to tell him some things."

Bologna Burgers, Anyone?

NASCAR drivers eat high on the hog these days, what with their salaries continuing to grow exponentially.

There is still room, though, for down-home delicacies like the bologna burger, one of Elliott Sadler's favorites.

Sadler once established a record of sorts at South Boston Speedway in Virginia, where he ate 16 bologna burgers in a six-hour period. He survived to tell the tale.

"I ate 16 bologna burgers, and they were all with onions and mustard and stuff like that," Sadler said. "I was a crew member for my brother, but I guess I wasn't doing much work on the car, because I was eating bologna burgers."

He made no plans to improve on his record.

"I can't eat like that anymore," he said. "I think when I was young I had a wooden leg or something and didn't gain any weight. Now I can't eat that much."

It's a Car! It's a Boat!

Dale Earnhardt Sr. and Ken Schrader were racing friends, traveling buddies, and fans of unique vehicles.

Dale Earnhardt Sr. and Ken Schrader were collectors of unique and rare vehicles, so when they saw a German-made Amphicar, similar to the one above, they had to purchase it.

It should surprise no one, then, that when they were traveling together on a trip to Detroit, they pooled their money and bought a sort of vehicle neither of them had seen: an Amphicar. The vehicle could be used on land and in water, and, when Earnhardt and Schrader got a look at it, they decided they had to have it.

"Dale gave the guy $500, and I called my shop and had a $10,000 check and a rollback [hauler] sent up to get it," Schrader said. "We got it back to North Carolina, and Dale told me not to put it in the water until he was there. Of course, we went back to the shop and drove it right in the pond out there. He drove by and got pissed."

The car later hit the water at nearby Lake Norman, much to the surprise of diners at a lakeside restaurant. Watching Schrader come up out of the water and drive into the restaurant parking lot had some people checking their drinks.

It's the Great Pumpkin, Darrell Waltrip

Darrell Waltrip is a NASCAR driving champion, a popular television commentator, and one of the most visible people in the motorsports community.

He also has a history with pumpkins.

It happened during Waltrip's teenage years, which, he acknowledges, were rowdier than most.

"I remember me and about five buddies loading into my old '55 Oldsmobile and heading up to a place called Reid's Farm," Waltrip said. "Man, I was proud of that Olds. I called it the 'Blue Goose' because I had painted it blue with a paintbrush. Out at that farm, they grew these tremendous pumpkins. We got a couple and headed back to the drive-in where everybody went. People would drive in there and show off, you know, spin their wheels or something like that.

"We smashed a couple of those big pumpkins at the drive-in entrance and made the biggest, gooiest mess you ever saw. Cars would come flying into the drive-in and start skidding. Right next door was a record shop, and three cars crashed into the building that night."

What about the other pumpkin?

"This guy came up beside us and started tossing water balloons," Waltrip said. "So I picked up this pumpkin and heaved it out the window at the guy's car. The thing went right through the windshield. So there's that guy sitting in his car with the windshield and pumpkin in his lap."

Perhaps wisely, Waltrip moved on.

An Aunt or an Uncle?

Before NASCAR's so-called "Car of Tomorrow"—introduced in 2007—brought significant changes to the landscape, manufacturer decisions to bring new racing models to the circuit often stirred criticism.

Model changes had to be approved by NASCAR, which would give a thumbs-up or thumbs-down to body modifications proposed by manufacturers. It wasn't surprising when teams aligned with one camp would oppose car changes proposed by another, and NASCAR often was caught in the middle.

In July 1997 Ford introduced its new racing Taurus, a car designed to replace the Thunderbird. Immediately, Chevrolet teams, which were racing the Monte Carlo model, were critical of the new car, and Chevy team owner Felix Sabates was perhaps the most outspoken.

"After looking at it, I don't know why they spent so much time working on it," Sabates said. "It looks like to me all they did was take a Monte Carlo and put a Ford nose on it. If that's a Taurus, my aunt is my uncle."

Hey, Not So Fast, Bud

As NASCAR racing became more popular in the 1990s and crowds at racetracks mushroomed, drivers and other racing-team members worked on methods and routes to leave speedways quickly after races, in order to avoid many of the traffic nightmares fans face.

Former team owner Bud Moore of Spartanburg, South Carolina, was one of the players most interested in making a hasty exit from race sites in the few minutes after an event. His exit speed didn't go unnoticed in the garage, which frequently is a hotbed for jokesters.

"They got him pretty good one year at Martinsville," remembered Donnie Wingo, who worked for Moore's team for 10 years. "Henry Benfield [a longtime NASCAR mechanic] stuck a jack up under his car. He was always trying to get out real quick. As soon as the gate opened, Bud was going to take off and get out of there. He jumped in the Lincoln. The tires started spinning, and he was sitting there going nowhere.

"We were all standing there watching and laughing."

So, How Did They Go?

The inaugural Southern 500, held on September 4, 1950, was the first asphalt race in NASCAR history, the first 500-miler, and the first in an unknown speed environment.

None of the drivers who showed up at the brand-new Darlington Raceway in the tobacco country of South Carolina had a clue what to expect. The track was banked, and the asphalt surface was a huge unknown. No one knew if stock cars could run 500 miles in competition.

Yet the response was remarkable. The field swelled to 75 cars, and the drivers included such giants as Fireball Roberts, Lee Petty, Tim Flock, Cotton Owens, Red Byron, Curtis Turner, and Buck Baker. On race day, a throng of fans converged on the relatively remote track; some estimates of the crowd size reached 20,000.

The race lasted six hours and 38 minutes, and Johnny Mantz, a successful midget racer, was the marathon winner, in large part because he ran a steady pace and preserved his tires.

On such a long day in the drivers' seats, one of the primary concerns was what would happen when nature called.

"Some of them fixed a rubber hose down through the floorboard of the car with a funnel on it," driver Jack Smith said. "We had never run four or five or six hours."

A Fortunate Awakening

Longtime NASCAR public-relations official and historian Bob Latford saw many unusual things in decades of following the stock-car-racing circus around the country.

Latford, who died in 2003, was around NASCAR racing virtually his entire life. He sold programs for races on the Daytona Beach, Florida, beach-road course in the 1950s and saw the sport grow into the national success it became in the 1990s.

Among the many oddities Latford encountered during his long career was one he remembered from the old beach-road course.

"I was in the south turn there for the race," Latford said, "and they had taken a motorgrader to smooth the turns. The grader had left big tire tracks on the top of the turn. Bill France Sr. [NASCAR's founder] was driving and inspecting the track. He noticed something irregular. Some guy had gone to sleep in the rut the motorgrader had left, and the sand had virtually covered him.

"France woke him up."

A Very Fast Race-Winner

Retired driver Buddy Baker was one of NASCAR's best on the circuit's biggest tracks, but he came up short year after year in the Daytona 500, the sport's biggest race, before finally scoring a victory in 1980.

It was a magical moment in Baker's long and successful career, but his celebration was relatively short and sweet. After victory-lane excitement and a string of winner's interviews, Baker retired to his motel.

"I went to bed," he said. "I didn't even go to a party or anything. I had to drive home, because I had to be in Richmond in a couple of days, so I went to bed. After two hours, my eyes [were] still wide open, so I said, 'You might as well get up and go home.'

"So, I packed up everything and took off. Just as I entered the wonderful state of Georgia, I topped a hill. Nobody on the road, 2:30 in the morning, I topped a hill, and the Fuzzbuster looked like it was dancing on the dash. I went, 'Oh, no,' and I looked at the speedometer, and I went, 'Holy Jeez.' So I pulled over, and the guy came up, and he said, 'Buddy Baker! I can't believe it. I am such a fan of yours, but you have the worst luck, and this is one of those times.'

"I was sitting there thinking about the Daytona 500 and what it meant. I had just spent the whole day running 200 miles per hour. I was so excited and happy that it didn't even bother me. So you got a speeding ticket. You won the Daytona 500, too."

Checks and Chicken Bones

NASCAR moved its Cup-series awards banquet to New York City in 1981 to put its champion driver and other leaders of the sport in front of the movers and shakers in the world's corporate hub.

That move has been a success, and, although there occasionally is talk about moving the banquet (to Las Vegas, for example), Manhattan has been a worthy host.

Prior to the move to New York, the banquet was held at the old Princess Hotel in Daytona Beach, Florida, near NASCAR headquarters, and it was certainly far from the black-tie affair of modern times.

"The behavior of individuals at banquets in those days would be totally unacceptable now," remembered longtime NASCAR official Jim Hunter. "Les Richter [a former NASCAR executive] would practice throwing chicken bones across the room. He'd pick out a pal across the way and just toss them. And the big prize then might have been a Regal Ride jacket with the driver's name on it."

See? It's Right Here on the Door

It is no surprise to most race fans that hotel-room prices in almost every city hosting a race weekend are increased to rates that often seem ridiculous.

It's simple supply-and-demand, the hotel operators say, but it hardly seems fair to fans that they're paying $200 a night for a $50 motel room.

Although drivers stay in motor homes at most tracks these days, before the arrival of those million-dollar living rooms on wheels, teams also fought the hotel-motel battle.

Earl Parker Sr., a longtime Champion Spark Plug Co. representative who traveled NASCAR roads for decades and became one of the garage area's most popular regulars, came up with a unique solution to the problem during a race-weekend trip to Long Pond, Pennsylvania, for a race at Pocono Raceway.

Startled by the elevated prices at the hotel where he was staying, Parker noticed that the hotel's normal rates were listed on the hotel-information-and-rates sheet that is placed on the main door in most hotel rooms.

So Parker did what any normal person would do. He removed the door from its hinges, hauled it down to the front desk, and announced to the clerk that he would be paying the price listed on the door and not a cent more.

Let's Try Winstons, Not Camels

Before the R.J. Reynolds Tobacco Co. and its Winston cigarette brand signed up to become NASCAR's primary sponsor early in the 1970s, NASCAR founder Bill France Sr. and his son, Bill, later the NASCAR president, had meetings with various R.J. Reynolds officials.

One of those occurred before anyone had mentioned the possibility of R.J. Reynolds promoting the entire series.

"Senior and I went to a meeting with them in Winston-Salem [R.J. Reynolds' headquarters]," France Jr. remembered. "He suggested that they bring a camel [R.J. Reynolds made Camel cigarettes] over to the racetrack in Winston-Salem and do some kind of promotion.

"They said, 'You don't want camels. They're nasty, and they'll spit at you. You don't want camels.'"

That could be why Winston—and not Camel—ultimately became NASCAR's major sponsor.

Experience Counts

Being a rookie in any sport isn't easy. In NASCAR racing, it can be particularly tough because there is so much to learn so quickly and at so many different places.

What to do? Can you seek help from a veteran? Well, maybe.

"The first thing they'll tell you is that it's impossible, that you'll never beat us anyhow," said retired driver Buddy Baker. "They'll also say that by the time you get good enough to beat us we'll be retired anyhow.

"I once asked Curtis Turner where you backed off going into a corner at Hillsborough [North Carolina speedway]. Well, when I got to that point I might as well have kept it wide open because I wasn't going to make it through the corner anyway. I went backward through the gate and into the parking lot.

"I came back in and said, 'Hey, are you sure you drive it in that deep?' He said, 'Yeah, but I've got 20 years' experience.'"

Like Ships Passing in the Night

Before chartered planes ferried NASCAR crew members around the country, teams used a variety of transportation to travel the circuit.

In the 1970s Virginia team owner Junie Donlavey used a large bus to move his team from track to track. He usually rode along.

On a trip from Donlavey's shop in Richmond, Virginia, to a race weekend at Talladega, Alabama, the bus stopped at a rest area near Mooresville, North Carolina. Donlavey was asleep in the rear.

Everyone else walked off the bus to visit the restroom. Donlavey woke up a few minutes later, realized where he was, and left the bus to walk around.

The rest of the team returned to the bus and, not realizing their boss wasn't still asleep in the back, returned to the interstate. Donlavey walked back to the bus, only to find that the bus wasn't there.

Donlavey called a friend, driver Elmo Langley, to pick him up and give him a ride to Talladega.

The rest of the team? They were many miles down Interstate 77 before they realized they had lost a key passenger.

Tough Times on the Flagstand

Chip Warren was NASCAR's chief flagman from the mid-1970s into the early 1980s. The sport wasn't quite so structured and wasn't in full view of the unforgiving eye of television as it is today, and so there were more opportunities for pranks and practical jokes.

Warren often took advantage of those opportunities.

As with the current schedule, many of the races in those years used celebrity starters to drop the green flag, and they shared the flagstand with Warren and a backup starter for the first few laps of the race. Unfurling the green is a very public act, and many honorary starters are nervous. Warren was more than happy to prey on their fears.

"When the honorary starter got there, I'd always ask Doyle Ford [the other NASCAR official on the stand] if he had brought a pair of special shorts for the honorary starter," Warren said. "Jimmy Carter was the starter one year in Atlanta when he was campaigning for president. He was in the stand, and I asked Doyle that question. He said no, of course. Carter asked why I wanted to know about the shorts, and I told him, 'Well, when you throw the green flag, and the draft comes by, it can cause a rupture.' He said, 'What should I do?' I told him to cross his legs."

Of course, Warren was kidding. But his spiel was quite believable.

"I looked around, and there were two secret-service agents behind me," he said. "They both had their legs crossed."

"Don't Worry, Mate"

NASCAR ran a race in Australia in 1988 to test the waters for major-league stock-car racing outside of North America. The late Neil Bonnett was among the NASCAR regulars who participated in the event.

It was not Bonnett's first race activity in Australia, however. He had accepted invitations to the country several times before in the 1980s to drive at small ovals.

On Bonnett's first trip, he arrived at the track and encountered a couple of surprises. First, the cars were racing clockwise around the track, opposite of the direction he had raced. And the steering wheel on the race car he had been provided was on what Bonnett—and virtually every American—would consider the passenger side of the vehicle.

"Don't worry, mate," someone on Bonnett's crew said. "We'll fix it."

Bonnett walked to a concession stand, ate a hot dog, and returned a few minutes later. He looked in the car to discover that the steering wheel had been moved to the left side of the car.

Bonnett hopped in the car and, in practice, ran into the first turn for the first time. As he turned the wheel, he noticed that it was making unusual clicking noises. The cause? The crewman had moved the steering wheel to the left side of the car, but, of course, the steering column remained on the right side. He had connected the steering wheel to the column by using a bicycle-type gearing chain.

It wasn't Bonnett's best race ever.

Watch Out for Marine Life

Retired drivers James Hylton and Richard Childress raced against each other for many years when both were basically struggling "independents," with little money to compete with the heavily financed teams.

Hylton and Childress remained reasonably competitive, however, and they also developed a close friendship, one that was famous in the garage area for producing practical jokes. Some were too wild and crazy to be shared in print.

"I locked him in the back of a truck one race morning," Childress said. "We let him out when most of the drivers were in the cars. He was sweating when he came out of there. Another race—we used to run those old Ford Econoline [van] seats in the cars. I opened up a can of sardines and slid it underneath the wires under the seat. Man, that thing was smelling bad when she started getting hot. And I put a crab in his car one year at Dover."

Hylton gave as good as he got.

"Everybody used to race with a gallon Thermos jug in the car," he said. "I got to his when they weren't looking one year in Darlington and put a bottle of liquid laxative in it. I mean, I dumped the whole thing in there. They had port-a-johns near the pits then, and I saw him make a pit stop and run for it during the race."

Sterling on a Streak

Most NASCAR drivers are heroes in their hometowns, and Sterling Marlin is no exception. The folks in Columbia, Tennessee, and his former classmates from Spring Hill High School are proud to call Marlin one of their own.

Marlin, who followed his father, Clifton "Coo Coo" Marlin, into stock-car racing, seems to know almost everyone in and around Columbia, in large part because he still lives in the area. His buddies from high school still stop by Marlin's farm to talk about the old days.

One of the stories that's frequently repeated involves a streaking incident that included Marlin and several of his classmates.

Marlin, his friend Tony Williams, and three other Spring Hill students decided to streak one of the local hangouts, Stan's Restaurant. Perhaps predictably, Marlin drove the getaway vehicle—a 1972 Chevrolet pickup. Williams rode inside the truck with Marlin. The three streakers were in the bed of the truck.

They sprinted through the restaurant quickly, providing some quick entertainment for a postgame football crowd, then Marlin gunned the Chevy and roared off into the night. He said he still remembers the sight of his friends' rear spoilers bobbing in the darkness in the back of the truck.

"It was one of the funniest things you'd ever want to see," he said. "The moon shining, I guess you'd say."

The streakers were fortunate that Marlin didn't depart early and leave them high and dry.

Those Diamonds Would Be Huge

Jake Elder, one of racing's most inventive crew chiefs, picked up the nickname Suitcase Jake because he changed jobs virtually every time a calendar page flipped.

Elder worked with some of the greatest drivers in NASCAR history, including David Pearson, Darrell Waltrip, and Benny Parsons. And he was crew chief—for only a while, naturally—for a young driver named Dale Earnhardt.

After Earnhardt scored his first career victory at Bristol, Tennessee, in 1979, Elder tossed him one of the great quotes in NASCAR history: "Stick with me, kid, and we'll both have diamonds as big as horse turds."

By the next season, Elder was gone, but his quote lives on. And Earnhardt did wind up with enough money to buy virtually any diamond size he wanted.

Okay, You Fans, Put 'Em Up

Darrell Waltrip won the NASCAR Cup in 1982 and accumulated 12 race wins along the way.

One of the most memorable "DW" moments from that season, however, occurred on one of his worst days. When Waltrip crashed hard in the World 600 at Charlotte Motor Speedway, thousands of fans cheered wildly, which sent Waltrip into an unusual tirade.

Waltrip invited the fans to meet him "in the Big K [store] parking lot at a certain time, and anybody who doesn't like me can show up, and we'll just duke it out. I really don't think they cared whether I was hurt or not. I'm embarrassed for the sport. It might have been an indicator of the mentality of a race fan. It's a disgrace.

"Maybe the fans are disappointed because nobody's had a bad wreck lately. I would hate to think that I could have a kid in the stands seeing the way the people act. I would never take him back to a race."

There were no reports of Waltrip and any fans actually dueling at the Big K—or anywhere else.

Thunderbird or Underbird?

Lowe's Motor Speedway near Charlotte, North Carolina, has a long history of unusual promotions.

In 1983 a relatively innocuous plan almost turned into trouble. The track announced that the winner of the pole position for the October race that year also would win a Ford Thunderbird, or, as it was described on the race entry blank, "a $15,000 Ford car."

Tim Richmond, who won the pole, wasn't satisfied with the prize. Instead of a new car, Richmond was presented with a Thunderbird that track officials had driven for 14,000 miles.

The next day, Richmond and track president Humpy Wheeler had a heated argument about the car, and the situation became so tense that they had to be separated by NASCAR officials.

Still, the promotional angle worked for Wheeler. He and Richmond later appeared together for a photo opportunity wearing boxing gloves.

Cops Converge on Turn 4

NASCAR fans are typically a rowdy bunch, and none are rowdier, collectively, than the thousands who gather at Talladega Superspeedway for Cup-race weekends twice a year.

Although law-enforcement personnel have toned down activities considerably in recent years, the Talladega infield remains one of the biggest and baddest party headquarters in NASCAR racing. And the huge campgrounds surrounding NASCAR's biggest track also are jammed with celebrating race fans all weekend.

Still, it was a little surprising when a NASCAR fan got a little too close to the racing on a Talladega race day in May 1986.

The start of the Winston 500 that year was delayed when a 20-year-old fan jumped in the Pontiac pace car and took it for a spin on the track. Talladega County Sheriff's Department vehicles gave chase in squad cars and on motorcycles, and the fan finally was nabbed when he was stopped by a roadblock in the fourth turn.

Pace-car keys have been watched a little more closely since that episode.

A Quick Comeback

Three-time Cup champion Cale Yarborough signed thousands of autographs during—and after—his driving career. Most of those signature meetings flashed by in a few seconds, but, occasionally, one stood out.

Walking through the Charlotte Motor Speedway infield one race weekend in the 1970s, Yarborough was approached by a young boy seeking an autograph.

"I'm one of your biggest fans," the boy said, handing Yarborough a drawing to sign. The boy said he had drawn the illustration, which showed Yarborough's car on the track trailing the cars of Richard Petty and Bobby Allison.

"If you're one of my biggest fans, why did you draw Richard Petty and Bobby Allison in front of me?" Yarborough asked.

"He said, 'Oh, no, man. Them cats are a lap down,'" Yarborough said.

Booster Seat Confiscated

When NASCAR officials take illegal parts from a race car at a race site, they typically display those items in or near the NASCAR mobile headquarters in the garage area. Drivers and team members are free to stop by and investigate the "engineering expertise" of other teams.

At a California Speedway race in 2005, the grouping of illegal items included something very unusual—a large Ontario, California, phone directory.

Huh?

Turns out, the phone book was a gag. According to the NASCAR inspector's tag attached to it, the book was an "unapproved, improperly mounted seat-heightening device [booster seat]."

The phone book supposedly was taken from the Chevrolet driven by Bobby Hamilton Jr., who stands only 5'5".

Burton Asks Tough Questions

It was the sort of question Michael Waltrip doesn't get every day.

Waltrip was answering questions from news-media members in the Daytona International Speedway press box after winning a Gatorade Duel 150 race in February 2005 when a "new" reporter chimed in with a question from the infield media center.

"This is Bob Smith from Raleigh," he said. "We have some reports that the IRS audited you and that you owed $396,000. Would you like to comment on that?"

Waltrip, normally one of the most talkative drivers in the garage, was taken aback. Seated on the other side of the racetrack, he couldn't see the questioner.

"Uh, I have no comment on that," Waltrip said.

After a moment of silence, the "reporter" said, "This is Jeff Burton from the South Boston Herald, actually."

Burton was waiting for his own press conference to start when he decided to spring a trap on Waltrip.

Stewart's Fashion Sense Questioned

The 10 drivers who qualified for the NASCAR Chase for the Nextel Cup in 2004 traveled to New York City to visit various news-media outlets and make personal appearances the week before the Chase started.

One of those stops was the Live with Regis and Kelly television show, and the show's producers decided to make the drivers the stars of a men's fashion show. Each of the 10 was given a shirt or jacket to wear before they went down a fashion runway to appear on the show.

This concept didn't make many of the drivers exceptionally happy, but they went along with the idea.

Tony Stewart was given a very bright orange sweater to wear, and he put it on while grumbling something about it not being in the contract.

Ryan Newman, noticing Stewart's irritation, walked over to him and said, "*Orange* you glad you made it?"

Boxers or Briefs?

Robby Gordon had an announcement for the motorsports press corps gathered in Homestead, Florida, for the final race of the 2003 season.

He had a new sponsor for the 2004 Busch season, and it was Fruit of the Loom underwear.

There were smiles all around in the press-conference room, and it was perhaps only a matter of time before someone asked the most important question of the day: "So, Robby, boxers or briefs?"

Gordon, perhaps anticipating the question, was ready with a quick answer. "What if I say, 'Nothing today?'" he asked.

The reporter obviously wanted to withdraw the question, but it was too late.

Tony? Obnoxious?

Tony Stewart, one of racing's most outspoken drivers, generally says what he thinks, often without concern for what sort of trouble it might produce for him.

In comments that appeared in *FHM* magazine in the spring of 2002, Stewart told an interviewer that fans at Talladega Superspeedway were obnoxious.

At the next race at Talladega, Stewart was roundly booed during driver introductions. One fan in attendance painted his portable outhouse to resemble Stewart's race car.

Stewart was ready for the reaction, however. He walked across the stage for driver introductions wearing a T-shirt that read, "I'm an obnoxious Talladega race driver."

Muppets Banished!

It was one of the weirdest incidents in the long history of NASCAR's tie-ins with sponsors.

At Chicagoland Speedway in July 2002, individuals dressed as characters from the popular *The Muppet Show* television series were banned from the track because of a sponsorship conflict.

Driver Dale Jarrett and Miss Piggy posed next to Jarrett's new race car, which featured Kermit the Frog and Miss Piggy painted on the hood. The Muppets and NASCAR briefly teamed up to celebrate 25 years of the Muppets, until a sponsorship conflict caused a number of Muppets to be ejected from Chicagoland Speedway in July 2002.
Photo courtesy of AP Images.

In a promotion devised by Action Performance, which sold diecast models and other racing paraphernalia, images of several Muppets were placed on cars in that weekend's Cup race. The Muppet characters were to appear at the track in support of that initiative.

But Kermit the Frog, Miss Piggy, and several other Muppets were booted out of the track because of a dispute over a licensing agreement.

The dilemma wasn't funny for some of those involved, but some of the Muppets made the best of it. Several were spotted outside the track holding "We Need Tickets" signs.

And there were signs in the NASCAR garage urging officials to "Free the Muppets."

chapter 4

A Rebel and a Rowdy

Darrell Waltrip, pictured here in 1975, stormed onto the NASCAR scene in 1972. Though people didn't take to the newcomer's brash ways at first, it didn't take long for Waltrip to prove himself a true contender.

When Darrell Waltrip showed up at NASCAR's top rung of racing in 1972, nobody had ever seen anything like him.

He was bold and brash, odd traits for a young rookie driver who had stormed across Southern short-track circuits but had proved nothing in big-time racing. Yet Waltrip made it clear from his first years in the sport that he had big plans and didn't really care what stood in his way.

He fired crew chiefs, had on- and off-track confrontations with the sport's established stars, and generally went about the business of establishing himself as a name to be followed.

When his driving career ended in 2000, he had 84 victories and three Cup championships and had earned the respect and admiration of millions.

The Origin of the Man Called "Jaws"

How did three-time NASCAR Cup champion Darrell Waltrip, now a popular television commentator, get his nickname "Jaws"?

That came courtesy of Cale Yarborough, another three-time champion.

In the mid-1970s, as Waltrip was trying to make a name for himself in the sport, seasoned drivers like Yarborough stood in the way. Waltrip, a rebel of sorts with little outward respect for the way things were, delighted in verbally sparring and matching wits with the sport's veterans, in particular Yarborough.

Waltrip also drove his race cars into spots that occasionally produced trouble, and that produced responses from those who were on the receiving end of those problems.

Case in point: In the 1977 Southern 500 at Darlington Raceway, a bad decision by Waltrip resulted in a wreck that eliminated his victory chances and those of Yarborough. After the race, in the drivers' lounge, someone asked Yarborough what happened.

"Jaws! Jaws happened!" Yarborough exclaimed.

"You know, the man with all the mouth that drives No. 88."

That would be Waltrip.

The nickname stuck. The next month, at a race at Charlotte (now Lowe's) Motor Speedway, track president and promoter-extraordinaire Humpy Wheeler acknowledged the circumstances by having a dead shark displayed on the track's pit road at the end of a wrecker's hook.

There was no sign on the wrecker and no comment from Wheeler, but it was clear that he was trying to stoke the fire.

Richard Petty, Historical Marker

In 1992, the last season in which he scored a NASCAR Cup victory, Darrell Waltrip sat down to discuss some of the drivers he had raced against since his debut in the 1972 season.

Waltrip had beaten—and tangled with—the best, in a career that produced more than its share of controversy but also resulted in three national championships and the building of a huge fan base.

"I learned to race from Richard [Petty] and Bobby [Allison] and Cale [Yarborough] and David [Pearson]," Waltrip said, mentioning the names of drivers who were stars when he arrived on the scene. "I learned everything from that crowd. Richard was always quick to point out to me what I was doing wrong. He had a finger about twice as long as mine, a big ol' crooked finger, and he'd point it right in my face or poke it in my chest.

"Richard is like some of those old houses we have in Franklin [Tennessee, where Waltrip lived]. He's historic. We need to put a marker in front of him. He needs to be protected."

Waltrip at Home on Bullrings

Even after he retired from Cup racing and started a lucrative career in television, Darrell Waltrip ran a few lower-division races on short tracks.

He started his remarkable career at tiny bullrings and said he enjoyed racing on the shorter tracks even at the peak of his success.

"I like the short tracks, always have," Waltrip said. "They're the most fun. And they're the most challenging to a driver. The smaller the circle, the higher the intensity and the quicker you have to react and do things, because you're running in such a confined area.

"I like racing close at Martinsville. I don't like racing close at Daytona."

Darrell a Poor Substitute for Stevie

When Darrell Waltrip was having his greatest success in race cars, his wife, Stevie, was a major contributor.

Stevie, who home-schooled the Waltrips' daughters on the road, rarely missed a race. Before the cars rolled off pit road, she would tape a card with a Bible verse written on it onto the dash of Darrell's car as a bit of inspiration for the miles to come.

Dale Earnhardt Sr. heard of Stevie's scriptures and asked that she provide the same service for him. She quickly agreed.

"When she's not at the track, she calls me, and I write them down for Earnhardt," Darrell once said. "I hate putting 'I love you' on there."

Excuse Me, Sir, Please Sign Here

NASCAR drivers have been asked to sign autographs virtually everywhere and on virtually everything, including almost every body part, live ducks and other pets, mailboxes, saw blades, and U-Haul trucks.

Darrell Waltrip signed more than his share during a long driving career. Of the thousands of times he swirled his signature, one stands out, he said.

An emotional Darrell Waltrip hugs his wife, Stevie, in victory lane after winning the Daytona 500 on February 20, 1989. Photo courtesy of AP Images.

"It was in a Saturday night race at a little track somewhere in Virginia," Waltrip said. "There wasn't much security. People were roaming around all over the place, even with the race going on. They had a mandatory pit stop. Everybody pitted at the same time. You only had so much time to pit and get back out on the track.

"I come in, and my guys are changing tires. A guy walks over. He had a program and a pen. He says, 'Hey, can you sign my book?' I said, 'Go away.' He said, 'I got to be at work at 10:00, and I can't stay until the end of the race, and I've got to get this book signed.'

"So I signed it. He wasn't going to leave."

Leroy Waltrip Opened the Door

Leroy Waltrip had no real background in racing, so it came as something of a surprise when two of his sons—Darrell and Michael—developed into winning Cup drivers.

They became known as "Leroy's Boys."

"I was always interested in cars but had no racing experience before Darrell," said Leroy, who worked for Pepsi in Owensboro, Kentucky. "I was going to a few races [as a spectator] around home when Darrell was born, but that was it.

"When Darrell was about 10 years old, racing go-carts on parking lots was the big thing. So he had to have one. We worked out a deal and finally got him one. Then they built a nice go-cart track in Owensboro, and it just started going from there.

"It starts off slowly, and then gradually you're up to your neck and sometimes higher than that.

"Darrell always had a lot of natural ability to race, whatever it was. He raced tricycles, bicycles, whatever there was to race. He was always competitive and had a natural feel for a race car. We ran the old cars around home and then ventured out. Like the go-carts, it went from a little bit to a whole lot. It was pretty obvious it was going to happen for Darrell. It was what he always wanted to do."

chapter 5
The First Family

Kyle Petty, center, holds his trophy at Daytona in 1979. His grandfather, Lee Petty (second from left), was at the forefront of stock-car racing since its beginnings, and his father, Richard (second from right), did much to carry the sport in the 1960s. The Pettys can truly be considered stock-car racing's first family. Photo courtesy of AP Images.

Although the France family has been at the forefront of NASCAR development and growth since the sport's beginnings, the Pettys of Randleman, North Carolina, can be considered stock-car racing's first family.

There has been a Petty at the heart of the sport since the pioneer years. Lee Petty, the family patriarch, started the family racing business and ran to 54 victories and three championships. Richard, his son, followed and essentially carried the sport on his back during its growth years in the 1960s. He became a national icon and scored a record 200 race victories and seven championships. Kyle, Richard's son, also drove into victory lane and continued the family's tradition of being at the front and center of the sport. Sadly, Adam, Kyle's son, was killed in a crash at New Hampshire International Speedway before his dream of carrying the family's success into a fourth generation could be fully realized.

Richard Petty: A Team Driver at 12

Richard Petty, NASCAR's all-time victory leader, started competing in Cup races at the age of 21, which, considering today's youth-dominated motorsports culture, was almost old.

Petty had had some previous on-road experience, though, even at 12 years old.

Before the debut of the massive, sophisticated haulers that now are used to transport race cars and equipment around the country, most teams towed their cars behind other cars or trucks. Occasionally, this was a challenge.

"There weren't many interstates," Petty said. "We went through the mountains and all over all kind of roads. Daddy [Lee Petty, a three-time NASCAR Cup champion in the 1950s] pulled that race car everywhere. Sometimes when we were going through the mountains, I'd get in the race car—I was probably about 12 years old—and help him out. I'd crank the car and push Daddy up the hill so we could go through the mountains. If he needed brakes on the other side going down, he'd hold his hand up, and I'd put the brakes on."

Do What I Say, Not What I Do

There often is something of a disconnect between the drivers of NASCAR's modern era and the colorful early history of the sport. Kyle Petty, whose grandfather, Lee, and father, Richard, were stars in the sport, attempts to change that at every opportunity, promoting racing's history and the contributions of those who drove the same road many years ago.

Petty knows more about the sport's past than most of his peers because he literally grew up in racing and traveled to most of the NASCAR-circuit stops with his family as a child. He became friends with many of the drivers.

One of Petty's favorites from the old days was Bobby Isaac, the 1970 Cup champion. A North Carolinian, Isaac won 37 Cup races and was a star during the brief lifespan of the winged

Chryslers. He died of a heart attack in August 1977 while driving in a Late Model race at Hickory (North Carolina) Speedway.

"I always thought Bobby Isaac was cool," Petty said. "He was a nice guy. He was always very nice to me when I was a kid. Some of the drivers would hardly acknowledge you, but he always went out of his way to.

"Bobby had the words 'True Love' tattooed on the back of his knuckles. And he smoked. From the time I was nine years old, he used to tell me, 'Don't ever smoke, and don't ever do this [get a tattoo] to yourself. When you're a nine-year-old boy and somebody like Bobby Isaac tells you not to get a tattoo, you don't. You remember that stuff."

Petty: Racing Needs Top Dog

Richard Petty knows about stardom. As perhaps the most important figure in the history of stock-car racing, he had legions of fans. Even today, long after his driving career, fans still flock to him at racetracks, eager to get his autograph.

It is important, Petty says, that racing have a star, a key figure for everyone else to target.

"You've got to have a lead dog," he says. "You've got to have somebody out there for everybody to shoot at. Look at golf. When [Arnold] Palmer and [Jack] Nicklaus won everything, you read all about it. When they went off the board, there was a different winner every week, and you don't even pay attention to who is winning. Tiger Woods comes along and rejuvenates the sport.

"Go to pro basketball. It was a flat thing, and along comes Michael Jordan. He lifts it from a mediocre deal into a great big deal. Racing has been the same way. It gets in a lull, and somebody will come along. There's always going to be somebody to pick it up and keep it going."

It seemed only appropriate, then, that, even as Petty started the final race of his career at Atlanta Motor Speedway in 1992, a youngster named Jeff Gordon was making his first start.

Richard Petty always touted the importance of racing having a star, a person in the spotlight, and he himself occupied that spotlight for many years.

Petty Stops Having Fun—For a While

When you drive a race car seemingly forever, which is exactly what Richard Petty did, you're likely to accumulate an impressive list of injuries. And that's exactly what Petty did.

A short list: a broken neck—twice, broken shoulders, every rib broken at least once, back dislocated, both knees broken, and both feet broken.

So it wasn't unexpected that, in February 1988, after Petty was involved in a vicious, tumbling crash on the front stretch at Daytona International Speedway in the Daytona 500, his wife, Lynda, had a special question for him in the emergency room.

"I had always said that I would quit driving when I stopped having fun," Petty said. "After that wreck at Daytona, Lynda and all the kids walked into the room. She said, 'Are we having fun?'"

Some observers anticipated that the brutal Daytona wreck would cause Petty to retire almost immediately. Instead, he drove for five more seasons. He admitted later, though, that the crash was one of several key factors that pushed him along the route toward finally making the retirement decision.

The wreck occurred on Lap 106 of the Daytona 500. Racing in a pack of traffic, Petty lost control of his bright-red-and-blue Pontiac coming out of Turn 4. Phil Barkdoll's car hit Petty's car, and the Pontiac turned and spun five times on its nose, flipped over twice, and wiped out about 20 feet of fencing along the front-stretch grandstand. A sequence of photos from the dramatic crash shows fans in the first few rows of the grandstands running for cover.

After Petty's car finally came to a stop, it was slammed by Brett Bodine's car. Petty was not seriously hurt.

Hey, Bud, That's My Hair

Although Kyle Petty's hairline has been gently receding for many years, he has retained the long hair and ponytail that has been one of his signatures during much of his racing career.

Sometimes the ponytail gets him in trouble.

During the 1996 Brickyard 400 at Indianapolis Motor Speedway, Petty crashed hard in the fourth turn. Track safety workers raced to the scene, removed the shaken Petty from the car, and prepared to move him to an ambulance.

As they lifted Petty, he screamed in pain. A major injury from the crash? No. One of the track workers had stepped on Petty's ponytail as the crew lifted him onto a stretcher.

Kyle Petty's signature ponytail, clearly visible here in 2006, has not always been an asset.

Hand Doesn't Go There

Kyle Petty normally is one of the coolest, calmest customers on the NASCAR Cup circuit.

But even the most placid drivers occasionally blow their tops, and Petty did just that in August 2007 at the Watkins Glen, New York, road course.

After an incident on the track during the race at the Glen, Petty, frustrated, slammed his hand on a door inside the Petty Enterprises hauler and broke a bone. He missed several races because of the injury.

Was it a stupid move?

"That didn't even move the needle on stupid for me," said Petty, who claimed a string of much worse "offenses."

Three Giants Go Out Together

Richard Petty, David Pearson, and Darrell Waltrip, three of the biggest winners in NASCAR history, were masters at avoiding wrecks in many situations where other drivers might have become victims.

In the 1978 Daytona 500, however, all three saw their cars crippled in the same incident as they were racing for the lead.

Sixty laps into the race, Petty's Dodge blew a tire as Waltrip and Pearson drafted closely behind him. Petty slowed, and Waltrip and Pearson couldn't decelerate quickly enough, and they all were pulled into a chain-reaction crash. Their cars dropped from the banking onto the infield grass and out of contention for the win.

The victory went to Bobby Allison, who won NASCAR's biggest race for the first time.

chapter 6
A New Face

Californian Jeff Gordon was clearly different from the average NASCAR driver when he rolled onto the scene in the early 1990s, but he quickly proved his salt and is now one of the sport's most beloved figures.

When Jeff Gordon rolled into NASCAR racing in the early 1990s, he brought a new personality and a new drive to the sport.

He was from California, not the South. He had grown up—literally—on go-cart and sprint-car tracks, not on Southern short tracks. He didn't fish or hunt.

He was different.

Yet it didn't take Gordon long to prove his worth. He scored his first victory in his second full season and logged his first of several championships in 1995. Over the course of the 1996, 1997, and 1998 seasons, he won a total of 33 races, forever solidifying his place as one of the sport's giants.

The Rivalry That Wasn't

The biggest NASCAR rivalry that never was matched Dale Earnhardt and Jeff Gordon.

Although fans of each driver desperately wanted the pair to race against each other every week with fenders banging and eyes on fire, Earnhardt and Gordon never really established a head-to-head rivalry. Their careers intersected for 10 seasons, including 1992, when Gordon ran only one race—his first—and 2001, when Earnhardt ran only one race—his last. They had very few on-track altercations, and they finished one-two in only seven races. Gordon won five of those.

Although many fans dreamed of a nasty, competitive divide developing between Earnhardt and Gordon, they instead were good friends and business partners. Each repeatedly expressed admiration for the other, and, as fellow Chevrolet drivers, they probably shared a little racing knowledge here and there.

Gordon surpassed Earnhardt's 76 career victories during the 2007 season and possibly will have a shot at topping Earnhardt's seven career championships.

A feisty competitor, Earnhardt was known to race people—including Gordon—even in practice.

"We had our times on the track where we had our disagreements," Gordon said. "We bumped and we banged. If he got into me, I might be mad about it at the time, but I'd get over it right away. If I got into him, it seemed like he'd get over it right away, as well. We didn't let those things linger on. It was racing, and some of that I learned from him, and some of it was just in my personality.

"There were times I wanted to speak my mind to him, and there probably were times he wanted to speak his to me, but that didn't happen after a race. We had a wreck in practice at Michigan. I never blamed him for it. It was just Dale. We were racing too hard in practice. I underestimated how hard he was wanting to race me. After the incident, I stayed away from him in practice. I didn't need any torn-up race cars, and I didn't see the need to race in practice."

Gordon said the only time the two discussed a racing situation was after an event at Pocono Raceway in the mid-1990s.

"I ran him down and got by him, and he got into the back of me," Gordon said. "We went into Turn 3, and both slid sideways up the track and lost two or three positions. I was pretty upset and thought it cost us a chance to win that race.

"A couple of weeks later, we were testing at Indianapolis. Somebody brought me a picture from Pocono. It was me coming straight at the camera. He was right on me. I'm sideways, and he's just stuffed up underneath me. You can almost see through the windshield to me. It was a cool photo.

"I said, 'I've got to have that.' I ran to his truck and threw it at him. I said, 'What do you call this?' I was just messing with him. I said, 'I've never asked you for an autograph. I want your autograph on this.' I still have that picture."

It became even more important to Gordon when the sport lost Earnhardt in February 2001.

Welcome to the Bigs, Boy

Dale Earnhardt often talked about having a lot of respect for Jeff Gordon when Gordon rolled into Cup racing in the final race of the 1992 season. Still, Earnhardt was known to teach rookies a thing or two, and Gordon got his lesson in his first full season in 1993.

"My first real valuable lesson was in 1993 when I was a rookie," Gordon said. "We were racing at Phoenix. He was a little better than I was. I was running ninth or 10th. He got underneath me, and I raced him really hard. We went into [Turn] 3, and—boom—I was in the wall. I remember that being a valuable lesson to me. I think that was a way for him to teach the rookie how things were going to be."

Perhaps it worked. Earnhardt and Gordon raced side-by-side for almost a decade with very few problems.

Gordon Signs and Signs and Signs

As NASCAR has grown, so have the demands on its drivers. In addition to racing, testing, and practicing, they have responsibilities linked to their sponsors and to the media. And then there are the fans.

Fans wait hours for the chance to simply meet or get a glimpse of their favorite racers. Autograph lines often stretch for blocks when drivers make scheduled fan-event appearances. Those lucky enough to get garage passes follow drivers from cars to team haulers in search of that one signature they need.

It's tough on the competitors, particularly the top drivers. Some can't travel from point A to point B without a knot of fans traveling with them.

Jeff Gordon learned to deal with the crush long ago. As with most drivers, he signs autographs as he walks, knowing that if he ever stops, he'll be tied up for a long time.

Still, Gordon understands the fan interest and the fact that they want to be close to their heroes. He tries to accommodate as many fans as possible, particularly the younger ones.

"I try to take care of the kids," he says, "I try to be a role model to let them see that you can be someone who is at this level and still can have a positive effect on people that you meet and take time for them. I'm not better than anybody else. I've just reached a certain level with a certain ability I have, and that puts me in the public eye. So I try to put myself in the place of people who are interested in what I'm doing.

"Fans are amazing. They literally will stand in line for hours just for an autograph. That amazes me. You have to respect them and the interest they show in the sport and the time they take to follow it so closely."

Earnhardt "Never Gave Up"

Even as Jeff Gordon was racking up Cup championships and consistently adding more and more shine to his résumé, he did so under the shadow of Dale Earnhardt Sr., a man whose accomplishments Gordon's will be compared to for the rest of his career.

Gordon, who was Earnhardt's business partner, said he had the ultimate respect for him on the track.

"You just had to be in awe of not only what he accomplished but who he was and the way people looked up to him," Gordon said.

"I got the chance to race side-by-side with him. I was fortunate even in '93, when we came in, because we had good cars, to race with him and learn a lot from him on the track. In '95 we went for the championship. I'd watched him race for championships before, but then I got firsthand what it was like battling with him for one.

"He was so good at knowing when to win and when to bring that thing home to get the points. There are some guys who just have a special knack for knowing how to get the most out of a car every time they're out there on the racetrack. He looked at the big picture.

"He knew where he could shine and where he just had to get all that he could. He never gave up. Never. It didn't matter whether his car was way off or if he was laps down. He never stopped driving the wheels off of that thing."

Gordon the New Pearson?

Virtually every type of professional sport produces its own sort of fan disagreements. Was Mickey Mantle better than Willie Mays? Was Johnny Unitas better than Bart Starr? Was Larry Bird better than Magic Johnson?

NASCAR racing is no different. Fans will argue for hours—possibly aided by an adult beverage or two—about the best racetrack, the best car make, and, of course, the best driver. Is it

Richard Petty? Dale Earnhardt Sr.? David Pearson? Cale Yarborough? Bobby Allison?

And where does Jeff Gordon, certainly one of the top drivers from the period beginning in 1995, fit into the overall scheme?

"He's right at the top," said Richard Petty, clearly a pretty good judge, as a 200-time Cup winner. "He's in the top three or four drivers that's ever been here. Just because he understands what's going on. He's a real versatile driver. He takes whatever circumstances are thrown at him and makes the best out of it. Everybody can't do that. He doesn't seem to get rattled when the team has problems. He's pretty level-headed. He understands what it takes for the car and for him.

"He's pretty low-key, like David Pearson. He comes in and does his thing. Sure, Jeff gets riled, and he does something, but two minutes later he's off to something else."

Gordon a Gunner at Daytona

What makes a superstar driver? Victories, of course, and championships. But the way those are accomplished also has much to do with the way a driver is measured, and, in those cases, Jeff Gordon truly is a superstar.

In the season's most important race, the Daytona 500, Gordon made courageous—and outrageous—passes in 1997 and 1999 to emerge victorious. He made both of the moves late in the races, entering the first turn, and both were remarkable because they were at high speed, they were in high-risk situations, and they were with big money on the line.

In 1997, with a few laps remaining, Gordon smoked past Bill Elliott on the deep, deep inside of the first turn, his Chevrolet going low enough to open a new lane and possibly scare a few guys drinking beer in the infield.

Two years later, Gordon pulled a similar move on Rusty Wallace in almost the same place with the 500 trophy on the line, and he made it stick, cruising to his second 500 victory.

Jeff Gordon stands next to the trophy after winning the Daytona 500 for the second time on February 14, 1999.

If there had been any doubts about Gordon's abilities in the heat of the moment, those two races erased them.

Golf Carts vs. Mules vs. Helicopters

Think drivers are fast on the racetrack? Watch them after the race as they try to beat fan traffic. That's when they make really dangerous moves.

Dale Earnhardt Sr. was perhaps the best all-time at this particular activity. Earnhardt dreaded postrace traffic, so he had all his ducks in a row for departure. Unless he won the race or had other postrace responsibilities, Earnhardt was gone in a flash. Someone driving a van typically met him as soon as his car pulled into the garage. Earnhardt hopped out and climbed in the van to join his family members, and it was off to the races. He had a change of clothes inside.

Many drivers leave tracks via helicopter these days, but that, too, has created a logjam of sorts as drivers and other key team members form lines at the track helipads.

"If your day has gone bad, you can't wait to get out of there in a hurry," Jeff Gordon said. "I have actually kind of slowed my pace down. Obviously, the helicopters are the fastest way to get out. But nowadays there seems to be a line at the helicopter pad, because even the fans are using the helicopters to get out.

"I usually have a golf cart or a mule or something to get me over to the helicopter pad, get on it, and go. I haven't driven out of a racetrack in a long, long time. It has saved on not getting a lot of [speeding] tickets."

Well, I Kinda Like Him

Almost every NASCAR fan has a favorite driver, and some even have a particular dislike for a certain racer.

Although Jeff Gordon is among the most popular drivers in NASCAR, he also has a devoted corps of nonfans.

Carolyn Bickford, who happens to be Gordon's mother, ran into one in the airport in Paris.

"Do you like racing?" the man asked Bickford after he learned she was from Charlotte, North Carolina.

"Yes," she replied.

"Do you go to races?" he asked.

"Well, once in a while," she said.

"Well, I like the racing," he said. "I root for anybody but Jeff Gordon."

"I didn't have a problem with that," Bickford said. "I don't expect everybody to like him. But he kept on and kept on, and he knew more about him than I knew about him. He went on for about 10 minutes. Then he said, 'Who is your favorite driver? Who do you root for?'

"I said, 'I don't think you want to know that.' He just looked at me and said, 'Oh, is it Jeff Gordon? Did I offend you?'

"I said, 'No, not at all. He may not be my favorite driver, but he is my son.'"

That brought a speedy end to the conversation.

I Want My Pizza

When Jeff Gordon won the first Brickyard 400 at Indianapolis Motor Speedway, the day was like a dizzying dream suddenly turned real.

Gordon's formative years were spent near Indianapolis, and, as he moved through racing's ranks, he watched the kings of open-wheel racing conquer Indianapolis Motor Speedway. While he was still a kid watching heroes like Rick Mears at IMS, he dreamed of winning a race at the sport's mecca.

Gordon did just that in 1994, earning the cheers of the thousands of Indiana residents in the track's sweeping grandstands as he roared under the checkered flag to claim victory in the first Brickyard 400, a historic moment for NASCAR.

The rest of that first Brickyard 400 race-day was a whirlwind as Gordon moved from victory lane to interview after interview and to a celebration with his team.

Finally he made it to the Speedway Motel adjacent to the track to spend the night. His first priority was food.

"All we could think of was to order something," Gordon remembered. "I thought about pizza. I don't always care if it's the healthiest thing in the world. I just wanted something good. Pizza Hut. I called them and said I wanted to order a pizza to the Speedway Motel. The guy laughed and said it would be two hours because they couldn't get to me [due to the volume of traffic]. I said, 'I know. I'm Jeff Gordon. I just won that race, and I'm hungry,'" he said.

"They were like, 'Hold on a second.' They didn't believe me for a minute. The manager got on the phone. He said it would be a while before they could get it delivered. The front desk called the room and said that Pizza Hut had called to confirm that I was there. They were there in 25 minutes. I gave the guy a $100 tip."

And the pizza? Pepperoni, mushrooms, and pineapples.

chapter 7
Watch Your Step

After a terrible accident at the Busch Clash in Daytona, Ricky Rudd went on to win the Miller High Life 400 at Richmond two weeks later with his eyes literally duct-taped open.

Although innovations like "soft walls" and improved head and neck restraints have made racing much safer in recent years, it is clear that the world of motorsports remains a dangerous profession.

Even the best can be touched by the madness of a moment, as evidenced by the death of superstar Dale Earnhardt in the Daytona 500 in 2001. Each turn can hold a challenge, and drivers can't be certain what to expect from one lap to the next.

The danger is out there.

Racing with Eyes Wide Shut

Could a driver with eyes practically swollen shut win a NASCAR race? It happened in 1984 at Richmond International Raceway in Virginia.

Ricky Rudd, a Virginia native, had been hurt while racing in the Busch Clash—now the Budweiser Shootout—at Daytona International Speedway. That nonpoints race was the first event of the new season, and Rudd opened with a flourish. Another car hit his Ford in Turn 4, and the Ford spun sideways and went on a wild, airborne ride. It was one of the most spectacular crashes in the speedway's long history and often is replayed via videotape when memorable Daytona accidents are recalled.

"I spent the night in the hospital," Rudd remembered. "They wanted me to spend a few more nights, but I basically convinced them to let me go early. The only actual damage I had was torn cartilage in the rib cage. But all of the capillaries in my eyes had ruptured from the G-force of swinging the body around. There was just a lot of trauma—face swollen, and I was bruised and battered pretty bad.

"Fortunately, we came back and won the race the next weekend [after Daytona] at Richmond. It took a little assistance from duct tape to tape my eyes open so I could see where I was going, because my face was swollen."

Vickers: It's Not Checkers

Brian Vickers rolled into NASCAR Cup racing full-time in 2004 after success in the Busch Series, and it was assumed that he would make noise rather quickly.

He did, occasionally wrestling for positions in tough circumstances. Perhaps inevitably, he crossed swords with Tony Stewart, which resulted in some in-your-face discussion between the youngster and the established veteran. Vickers didn't cower in the corner.

"I think everybody has had a run-in with Tony," Vickers said. "Tony is a very aggressive driver. He and I had our battles, but I think the good thing about it is that there came a mutual respect out of it. He understood and respected where I came from and my position and that I wasn't going to back down.

"Some people don't understand. They can watch TV and say, 'You shouldn't have done that. You shouldn't get that upset.' You know what? When your life's involved and you're running 200 miles an hour, it's a dangerous sport. Everybody's going to handle it differently, and there are going to be emotions involved. There are going to be times when you have to stand up for yourself and put your foot down.

"We're not playing checkers. This is life-or-death stuff."

Dirt Tracks and Bloody Hands

Jack Smith was one of NASCAR's pioneers. He started driving in the sport's first season—1949—and won 21 races in a career that stretched from the pockmarked dirt tracks of the early days to the superspeedways of the 1960s.

Smith, who lived in Spartanburg, South Carolina, died in 2001 but lived to see the sport he helped to develop become something he couldn't have imagined. Almost everything, including the drivers, was different from the dust-covered beginnings of racing.

"There's very few of the drivers today who would have been successful back in the old days," Smith said. "They don't know how tough it was to get out of a car and blood be running out of your hands. You didn't want to do it, but if you wanted to make a living, you had to keep going.

"I don't think they could sleep in a car all night at some track and then race it and then tow that car from Charleston, South Carolina, to Jacksonville, Florida, to Savannah, Georgia, to Martinsville, Virginia, and run at all those places. I don't think there are many of them who love it enough to stay with it. Most of them are in it for the money and the glory. Back then you were in it because you loved it."

Smith ran almost everywhere and raced almost everything. In the end, he wound up in the Hall of Fame.

Riverside Crash a Hurdle for Labonte

Terry Labonte's career was one of the best in NASCAR history. He won two national championships and built a consecutive-race-start streak that peaked at 655, earning him the nickname Ironman.

Not everyone knows how close Labonte came to never reaching those numbers. He could have retired in 1982 after a frightening crash on the road course at Riverside, California, when he was only 26.

As he entered Turn 8 at Riverside, Labonte's car apparently cut a tire, and he sailed into the wall at near-full speed. Some observers figured he was at least seriously hurt, maybe worse.

"It's the fastest part of the track," Labonte said. "I thought, *Man, I'm going to hit that wall.* But I don't remember hitting it. I was knocked out a good while, I guess. I remember having a hard time breathing when I came to. Then I saw all that blood. Mine."

Labonte had extensive facial cuts, which required plastic surgery. He broke his right foot and left ankle and fractured several ribs.

Labonte returned to driving the next season but later said he would have quit after the Riverside wreck if his wife, Kim, had asked.

"If she had come into the room and asked me to quit, I would have," Labonte said. "I would have regretted it later. But, if she had said anything, I would have quit. I was hurting that bad at the time."

Cotton Owens: A Man of Vision

Cotton Owens had a spectacular career in auto racing, driving and building cars from the late 1940s (before there was a NASCAR) to the mid-1970s.

Like most other longtime drivers, however, Owens had his brush with death. Most successful racers have confronted the Big Wreck at some point in their careers. Owens crossed that bridge—barely—during a modified race at a fairgrounds track in Charlotte, North Carolina, in 1951.

As Owens drove to first place on the backstretch early in the race, driver Willie Thompson crashed his car on the other side of the track, and it came to rest on its roof.

"I was on the back bumper of Fireball [Roberts] about to lap him," Owens said. "Fireball went around Willie. Then people came running out on the racetrack [toward Thompson's car]. I could do anything with a race car and knew I had to do something quick. I flipped the car sideways and was going to go around the other side of Willie, but I had forgotten about two cars I had just passed. One of them hit me in the left door and turned me straight through Willie's car. I tore his car in half and went on through it and ran head-on into the bandstand [beside the track]."

Owens' face hit his car's steering wheel hard, and he was rushed to a Charlotte hospital, along with Thompson.

"My face was knocked sideways, and half of my teeth were out," Owens said. "My face was swelling, and I was having trouble seeing. Willie was in there in the hospital screaming at the top of his voice to do something for me. They took me over to another hospital, and I stayed there a couple of months.

"They wired up some bones in my cheek. They did the best they knew how back then."

Owens returned to racing in a few months and drove for another decade, despite the fact that problems with his left eye bothered him through the rest of his career—and beyond.

Owens said he had double vision and had trouble with depth perception, problems that eventually chased him from the driver's seat.

"When I was driving, I just let my right eye override the left," he said. "I would just squint it to where I was actually just driving with one eye. I enjoyed racing so much, it didn't bother me."

Plane Crash Wakeup for Roush

Jack Roush, the operating owner of one of the most successful teams in NASCAR racing, sees every day he lives as a bonus.

Roush was on the edge of death in the spring of 2003 when he crashed a small one-seat airplane into a lake in Alabama while on a recreational outing. Larry Hicks, a retired marine who happened to see the crash from his lakeside home, jumped into the water and rescued Roush, and, after a long period of recovery and rehabilitation, Roush now lives a more-or-less normal life.

Part of Roush's rehabilitation time was spent in the University of Michigan Hospital in Ann Arbor, and it was there, he said, that he realized the good fortune he had had in his life.

"I was exposed to two 24-year-old young men there," Roush said. "Both of them were paraplegic as a result of accidents. One of them was just out of college and getting his life started, and the other was just about to graduate within a couple months. One had a motorcycle wreck, and the other had some sort of four-wheeler, recreational wreck. Their lives were dramatically altered based on their injuries.

"There was a young woman there, less than 30 years old. She didn't have her children yet, but she had an accident and lost both of her hands above her wrists and both of her feet below her ankles. She had four stubs, and they were teaching her how to walk. She was educated, she was articulate, she had her life in front of her.

"I was 60 years old. I had celebrated a 60th birthday. I'd raised three kids. I'd had a lovely wife. I'd had just a great chance to do many things I couldn't have dreamed that would make up my life as a youngster. But if I could have given those two young men their legs back and that young woman her hands and feet, they could have left Jack in the water. I would have been just fine. Anyway, those are the things that have affected me."

Irvan's Career Remarkable

Ernie Irvan wrote one of the most remarkable stories in the history of NASCAR racing.

Almost killed in a brutal crash at Michigan International Speedway in August 1994, Irvan survived, went through a long rehabilitation, and returned to racing in October 1995. He also returned to victory lane.

A second hard accident at MIS in 1999, however, pushed Irvan into retirement. In an emotional press conference at Darlington Raceway on September 3, 1999, he announced that he was leaving the driver's seat.

"Everything that I've done and been able to accomplish in the sport has made me decide that the smartest thing I can do is look

Ernie Irvan wipes a tear from his face as he announces his retirement from NASCAR at an emotional press conference at Darlington Raceway on September 3, 1999.

to the future and retire," Irvan said as his wife, Kim, and their children sat beside him. "A lot of times, financially, you can't retire. I'm able to make that decision and make it smart.

"Obviously, being able to come back and drive again [after the first accident] was a dream come true. It's still a dream. Winston Cup racing is something I love to do, but I know it's smart for me to say, 'Hey, I don't want to push the envelope.' I'm 40 years old, and my experience in Winston Cup racing has been very good, and there's no doubt that I don't want to push the envelope.

"There are a lot of things Ernie Irvan can do for his career, but, hey, right now I'm going to hang it up as a driver."

Kim Irvan says her husband was like "a cat with nine lives, and he has used eight of them. It was a miracle in 1994, and most people don't get one miracle."

Irvan has remained involved on the fringes of racing and makes appearances at races several times a year.

Drive 'Til You See the Can

How do drivers know when to back off their speed entering a turn? In the old days, they often chose a telephone pole or a track post and cut their speed at that marker. Sometimes the dust was so bad drivers would pick out a fan wearing a bright shirt in the grandstand, but that tactic failed—obviously—when the fan went for a hot dog.

Still, the trick of driving a car as far into the turn as possible at full speed makes for faster laps, and all drivers find their way differently. Looking for the edge of danger is an everyday task.

"When my uncle [the great Mario Andretti] was driving a Champ dirt car," said driver John Andretti, "my dad went out and put a can on the wall to show him where everybody was backing off. Well, whoever drove in the deepest, my dad would move the can down about a car length. Mario drove all the way down to the can and never lifted and got fast time.

"You have to key off certain things. That's what makes tracks like Martinsville and Richmond and places like that really tough, because it's hard to get a good mark on where to lift. So you have a tendency to overdrive going into the corner."

Spencer vs. Busch

When Kurt Busch rolled onto the NASCAR scene, he stirred the waters quickly.

One of the people hit by the waves was Jimmy Spencer.

When Busch knocked Spencer's car out of the lead and went on to win the March race at Bristol Motor Speedway in 2002, Spencer promised retaliation.

Kurt Busch gestures his disapproval at Jimmy Spencer after Spencer caused him to crash during the Brickyard 400 at the Indianapolis Motor Speedway on August 4, 2002. Photo courtesy of AP Images.

"I never forget," Spencer said. "The only thing is, when I smash back, he won't finish."

Later in the season, at Indianapolis, Busch crashed after contact from Spencer's car. Busch climbed out of his bashed racer and gestured at Spencer as Spencer drove past the crash scene. Later, Busch called Spencer "an old, decrepit has-been."

Spencer's bigger revenge came the next season when he punched Busch in the nose as Busch sat in his race car. That sparked all manner of talk in the garage area, but the problems between the two eventually faded.

Pearson Throws One

In 1999 *Sports Illustrated* named retired NASCAR racer David Pearson as its Driver of the Century.

That award led Spartanburg, South Carolina, Pearson's hometown, to hold a two-day celebration in Pearson's honor in May 2000. Numerous racing celebrities, including drivers Bobby Allison, Ned Jarrett, Jack Smith, and Dick Brooks and team owners Bud Moore, Cotton Owens, and Leonard Wood attended the festivities, which included a dinner, a Pearson roast, and a downtown parade.

Among the stories tossed around about Pearson was this one from Jarrett about a race in the early 1960s at Tar Heel Speedway in Randleman, North Carolina:

"David knocked me into the wall and messed my car up pretty bad. I was in the pits three or four laps getting it fixed. I caught back up to him on the racetrack. I hit him a lot harder than he hit me. When I came around the next lap, he was out of the car and had the steering wheel in his hand. He threw it at me. We never had any more trouble after that."

chapter 8

From Here to Eternity—Almost

Darlington Raceway is NASCAR's most unusual track, with its egg shape, odd banks, and tight lanes.

NASCAR has raced on virtually every sort of landscape imaginable—from the hard-packed sand of Daytona Beach, Florida, to the historic bricks of Indianapolis Motor Speedway to tiny bullrings in the backwoods to artificial courses carved out of airport runways.

The delight has been in the diversity. A successful NASCAR driver must excel on a wide variety of tracks. The only concrete similarity is that all have finish lines.

Plus, No Yellow Buildup

The dilemmas associated with big-time stock-car racing have sparked numerous types of inventiveness by drivers and mechanics over the years. Some of those efforts have been expensive and complicated, as teams spend many months and many dollars in intense research and development programs. They can spend hundreds of thousands of dollars chasing a few hundredths of a second.

And, with alarming regularity, teams cross the line between *approved* and *unapproved* in their searches for speed, sometimes coming up with nifty devices that surprise even the most veteran NASCAR inspectors. NASCAR collects and catalogues most of those devices, and its top officials continue to marvel at the depths to which some creative folks will go.

Then again, an on-track solution can be as inexpensive and simple as a floppy household mop.

The old beach-road course at Daytona Beach, Florida, staged some of the most spectacular races in NASCAR history. In the 1940s and 1950s, before Daytona racing moved to the huge new Daytona International Speedway several miles inland from the Atlantic Ocean, drivers raced with reckless abandon on the combined asphalt-sand course along the beachfront. The course was inviting to a particular kind of daredevil who would drive a fast car in all sorts of situations. The track also was unique in that its use was limited to certain times of the day. Can't race at high tide, you know.

Conditions were fine as drivers roared down the paved Highway A1A heading south, but when they made the left turn onto the hard sand portion of the course, chaos often erupted. Some drivers got too close to the water, became bogged down in the softer sand, and wound up in the surf. Others wound up wrecking in big piles of vehicles in the turns as drivers tried to maneuver through huge ruts in the sand.

As they raced north on the beach, sand, salt, and an occasional contribution by an on-target seagull pockmarked their cars' windshields and often made visibility—already less than perfect—very difficult.

Some drivers solved this problem by throwing a wet mop in their cars and, at a relatively safe juncture, reaching out the driver's window with the mop and cleaning the windshield.

They don't do that at 200 mph at Daytona International Speedway.

It Was a Matter of Locating the Dirt

Back in NASCAR's dirt-track days, the ability to see where one was racing and which competitor one was racing against wasn't a given. Flying dirt and mud often mixed with exhaust to make clear vision almost impossible for drivers. The dirt also could be challenging for spectators, some of whom no doubt took several showers after they arrived at home after the race. Many still carried some reminders of the track to work the next day.

Maurice Petty, Richard Petty's brother and a Hall of Fame engine builder for Petty Enterprises, also had a brief driving career. Richard became the family's driving star, but Maurice decided to try his hand at the wheel, too.

He experienced the vision problem in a dramatic way during a 1964 race at Occoneechee Speedway, a tough .9-mile dirt track in central North Carolina.

"The track was really dusty anyway," said Dale Inman, Richard Petty's crew chief. "When they started the race, the exhaust from the cars and the dust flying just made it practically impossible to see. It wasn't a problem for Richard, because he started on the front row, but Maurice was back there in the pack.

"There was a big wreck right there at the start with everybody piling into each other. They had to stop the race. Maurice missed the wreck, but he was complaining after they stopped the cars that he couldn't see. I went over to his car and cleaned off the windshield.

"Maurice said, 'I still can't see,'" Inman said. "So I cleaned off the inside of the windshield. 'Still can't see,' he said.

"It turned out he couldn't see because there was dirt all over the inside of his glasses."

Wait, Are They Starting without Me?

Although the current NASCAR Cup schedule is very crowded, teams competing before the so-called "modern era" sometimes raced several times a week, and the circuit had more than 60 stops.

That sort of wacky schedule produced some odd travel situations. Drivers ran in the Firecracker 400 at Daytona International Speedway in Florida on July 4, 1969. Two days later, they raced in the inaugural event at Dover International Speedway in Delaware.

The summer race at Daytona Beach now is a nighttime affair, but, for many years, it started late in the morning on July 4. In 1969 the teams ran there and then bolted for Delaware.

Many of the competitors were still trying to readjust their bodies when they rolled into Dover for the first Mason-Dixon 300.

"Everybody was laying around on benches and wherever they could get, trying to catch up on their sleep," said Dale Inman, then the crew chief for Richard Petty.

Enter Ray Melton, a legendary race announcer who was handling the public-address system for Dover's first race. Among other things, Melton was famous for the theatrical way he issued the "Gentlemen, start your engines" command.

Unfortunately, he jumped the gun and presented those famous words 30 minutes earlier than scheduled.

"Everybody was startled," Inman said. "Nobody was even in their cars."

The race wasn't exactly a classic. Petty won by six laps over Sonny Hutchins.

Score That One, You Guys

Darlington Raceway forever will be NASCAR's most unusual racetrack. Egg-shaped, oddly banked, and with tight racing lanes, Darlington has produced some of motorsports' most exciting events and, not surprisingly, some of its strangest.

Included among those is Johnny Allen's wild ride in the 1960 Rebel 300, a race which Joe Weatherly won.

Driving the 148th lap of the 219-lap race, Allen's car blew a tire as he rolled through the fourth turn. He hit the guardrail with full force, shot across the track, and sailed into the wooden stand that NASCAR used to house its scorers, collapsing part of the structure.

Remarkably, no one was hurt.

"I think there were a few of us that had to go change our underwear," said Morris Metcalfe, NASCAR's longtime chief scorer and timer. "Seriously, it did scare us, and some of us were a little shaken…. There was a cameraman standing on the front of the platform, and he received a small cut above his eye when the eyepiece popped him in the forehead. That was it."

NASCAR red-flagged the race so the scorers, a key part of every race prior to computerized scoring, could be relocated.

Because Allen's car had knocked out the stand's steps, track personnel brought a fire truck to the scene and raised the ladder so the scorers could leave the stand.

From Sea to Shining Sea

It is not a monument in the way that most people think of monuments, but a wall that stands on private property in Scotts Valley, California, represents a significant slice of the NASCAR story.

Bill France Jr., who was stationed in the area during a stint in the U.S. Navy in the early 1950s, received instructions from his father, "Big Bill" France, the founder of NASCAR, to contact an area racing promoter named Bob Barkhimer. Barkhimer controlled almost two dozen short tracks in California and had introduced much of the state to organized stock-car racing. France Jr. and Barkhimer met and talked, and among the eventual results was NASCAR's 1954 expansion to the West Coast and to 10 Barkhimer tracks. It was an important move for the France family's still-fledgling racing organization, one that gave it at least a veneer of national bearing and—perhaps as important—more quality places to race.

Only five years old, NASCAR could claim its reach stretched "from sea to shining sea."

France, who lived in Daytona Beach, Florida, sent Barkhimer some Atlantic Ocean seashells. When Barkhimer built a wall on his property in Scotts Valley, for many years NASCAR's West Coast headquarters, he used the shells in the mix. Atlantic had met Pacific. NASCAR stretched across the continent.

NASCAR's West Coast offices are now in the hustle and bustle of Los Angeles, but the link between the Frances and Barkhimer remains a solid one in the sport's historical context.

Daytona Doesn't Equal Talladega

Daytona International Speedway opened in 1959, and its sister track, then named Alabama International Motor Speedway and now Talladega Superspeedway, opened in 1969.

Because both tracks were giants—Daytona is 2.5 miles, Talladega 2.66 miles—and both were built by NASCAR founder Bill France Sr., the two usually were talked about as part of the same grouping. When they became the only NASCAR tracks to regularly require the use of engine-restrictor plates (because of excessive speeds), that pairing became even more pronounced.

There is a tendency for many fans to look on Daytona and Talladega as the same animal, then, and most drivers see that as a mistake.

Daytona requires a fine-handling race car, they say, while Talladega looks for power under the hood. And, although the draft

Daytona International Speedway, pictured here circa 2007, is one of only two tracks that require the use of engine-restrictor plates to curtail speeds during races.

is certainly a major factor at Daytona, it does not produce the huge, three-wide drafting packs for which Talladega is known.

"We equate the two because they are the places where we run restrictor plates, but there probably couldn't be any two tracks more different," said driver Dale Jarrett. "Talladega is wide. It was made for speed—big, sweeping corners, wide straightaways. If you get four-wide in the tri-oval, it's not a big deal. At Daytona, the track is much more narrow. The corners are sharper. In every Daytona 500 I've been in, the car that handled the best has won the race."

Innovation, Exploration, Confusion

The late 1950s and early 1960s opened a new era for NASCAR— and for its innovators—as superspeedway racing became a much more important element of stock-car competition. During the sport's early years, most of the racing had been done on tracks of a half-mile or less, and the wider and faster speedways being built brought on new challenges—and new opportunities. The giant new Daytona International Speedway opened in 1959. Bill France Sr. built the track as the stock-car answer to Indianapolis Motor Speedway. It was huge and high-banked, and it introduced NASCAR drivers and mechanics to a new universe.

Ask almost any driver his reaction to rolling through Daytona's tunnel for the first time and seeing the sheer size of the place, and it's almost always, "Wow!" or something unprintable.

No one knew what to expect. Cotton Owens was there the first year.

"When we started running Daytona, that was the beginning of really trying to streamline for wind resistance," he said. "We didn't know anything when we went to Daytona in 1959. No one knew you could go out there and draft faster with two cars than with one until we actually did it in the race. I set [a] fast qualifying time at 143 miles an hour, but that was absolutely a stock automobile, with a stock engine.

"Even at that speed, my car would actually raise the front wheels off the ground going in the corners. We didn't know how to keep it down. Of course, we learned. Dropping the front end down, raising the rear end. Went back in 1960, we were already dropping the front ends on them. Just learning from trying it. Somebody showed up with a car all propped up in the rear and ran fast, and it was on then. Everybody copied it."

Longtime mechanic Ray Fox Sr. said drivers were skeptical of Daytona's new speeds initially.

"But they got used to it," he said. "The cars handled better after a while. In 1960, when Junior [Johnson] won the race, he said it was amazing that he could catch a car's draft and pass them back with only a little 348-cubic-inch engine in a Chevrolet. He won the race with good common sense and good drafting."

Prior to that, no one in stock-car racing even knew what drafting was.

Hall of Fame mechanic Leonard Wood of the Wood Brothers team was one of the top innovators of his era—of any era. Shy and quiet, Wood nevertheless was on top of the game.

"Leonard made a lot of stuff with his hands," said David Pearson, who once dominated superspeedway racing in Wood Brothers cars. "He'd take the parking-light areas and bend them in a little, just for aerodynamics. They would do things like that. Anything to get the air to flow a little better."

Pearson, who retired from NASCAR racing with 105 victories, was involved in one of the most hilarious "cheating" stories in motorsports history. It happened at a Trans-Am race in the late 1960s as Pearson was driving for car owner Bud Moore on the road course at Riverside, California.

"[Bud] had a gas tank at Riverside that all the fuel wouldn't come out of when they drained it," Pearson said. "They had a thing up in it that would just let so much of it drain out. So the inspectors told Bud that he had to get all the fuel out of the tank before they came back. So he got a bunch of the guys on the team to stand around the car and pee on the ground so it looked like they had drained all the fuel out."

Occasionally, racing "innovation" was for no reason at all.

Noted engine builder Runt Pittman once worked for team owner Hoss Ellington. Pearson remembers Pittman screwing a hole in the intake manifold. Ellington, who enjoyed such chicanery but didn't necessarily understand all the applications, wanted to know why.

"Runt told him, 'Don't worry, it's something that's going to help,'" Pearson said. "Hoss couldn't wait to tell people about it. But Runt was just messing around with him. It didn't really do anything."

Magic in the Night

Bristol Motor Speedway is one of the most remarkable success stories in NASCAR racing.

Its two Cup races now attract more than 160,000 fans, and many more would buy tickets if they were available. At each event, particularly the night race in late summer, scalpers dance around the edge of the law and sell tickets for multiples of their face values. Bristol tickets have become objects of contention in divorce cases. Everybody wants to be inside to see what's going to happen.

It wasn't always this way at Bristol, however. Opened in 1961, the track struggled for years. The track had crowds of less than 10,000 for some of its early years, and the concrete grandstands, which could seat 22,000, looked pretty lonely.

In 1978 the track's August Cup race was moved from afternoon to evening. "We wanted something cool for the fans, cooler on the drivers, and something that would be a different spectacle," said Lanny Hester, then the track's co-owner. "We thought the night race would be a concept we could promote."

The change was greeted enthusiastically. The crowd size doubled for the first night race.

"It was one of the high points of my career, of my lifetime really, to be involved in something that was such a major turnaround," said Ed Clark, who was Bristol's public-relations director at the time. He now is president of Atlanta Motor Speedway.

"Forty-five minutes into the race, we were still turning cars around and sending them home," Clark said. "So the night thing made it kind of special. I don't know what it is, but it's turned into much more than a race. It's a cult happening."

When ESPN joined NASCAR and began showing Bristol's nighttime glow to the rest of the nation, interest in the track accelerated. Then, in the 1990s, new track owner Bruton Smith launched a building program that expanded seating by leaps and bounds. Now the bowl-shaped track has one of the biggest seating capacities in the country, and every seat is full.

A large part of the attraction is that the track's high banking guarantees speed—and action.

"Everything happens so fast at Bristol," said Bobby Labonte. "People just don't realize how fast we come out of those turns, and you really don't even have a chance to take a breath before you're thrown back up on the banking."

Tempers often flare at the track because it's so easy to become involved in wrecks. There seldom are one-car accidents at Bristol. It is theater-in-the-round taken to the absurd.

"You're going to leave here either mad or glad," said team owner Eddie Wood. "You know if you can survive it, you're going to have a good run. It can be a wreckfest, but it's one of my favorite tracks. Everybody's so close to you. The crowd is close. You can just feel it."

From Dust to Dust...

Martinsville Speedway, the biggest little track in auto racing, opened in 1947, two years before NASCAR began its top series.

The track, built in southern Virginia by local entrepreneur Clay Earles, who raised $60,000 for its construction, staged its first race on September 7, 1947. It was a financial—if not an artistic—success.

More than 6,000 spectators turned out to see the new game in town, and many of them came straight from church in their Sunday finest. That wasn't a good idea. When the green flag fell, the cars created a massive dust storm, which blanketed the track and virtually everything and everybody in the vicinity. "When the race started, it looked like someone had dropped a nuclear bomb," remembered Earles years later. Aware that dust could pose problems, Earles had coated the track surface with 20,000 gallons of oil, calcium chloride, and water, but all that was of little help.

Red Byron won the race and the $500 top prize.

Martinsville joined NASCAR in 1949 and was part of the first season of Cup racing. Byron, a World War II veteran who raced despite having suffered major injuries in the war, also won the first Cup race, which was held on September 25, 1949.

The track's continuing problems with dust convinced Earles that he should pave the track, which, in the 1950s, was unusual for a short Southern speedway.

"After the first race in 1947, for the next five years we didn't draw half that many," Earles said. "In 1955 I decided to pave the track. There were no paved tracks around. I was talking with Bill France Sr. [NASCAR founder and a close friend of Earles] about something else, and I told him I had decided to pave it. He said, 'Don't you think you'll ruin it?' I said, 'Well, Bill, if I don't pave it, I'm ruined. So I'm going to pave it.' And I did."

It was a smart move. Martinsville has remained a part of NASCAR's top series since that first season and reliably fills its towering grandstands.

And there's no dust.

Flipping Over Daytona

Racing on the famous beach-road course in Daytona Beach, Florida, in the 1950s attracted racers far removed from the Sunshine State. Word of mouth and newspaper and magazine stories carried information about Daytona's hard-packed sand and the exciting racing happening there, and soon daredevil drivers were arriving on Florida's east coast in virtual caravans.

Russ Truelove was one of those drivers, and his experience landed him in *Life* magazine—and on his head.

Truelove drove to Daytona Beach from Waterbury, Connecticut, in 1956 to drive in the beach-road race in a Mercury he had ordered from the Waterbury Lincoln-Mercury dealership. Truelove, the dealership's service manager, strengthened the car with a roll bar and numbered the outside of the car—No. 226—before driving it south.

It was an exciting time for Truelove, but it ended all too quickly.

Racing Jim Reed into the north turn of the asphalt-sand course, he drove into the softer sand, and the car started sliding and then flipped into the air.

"Once your front wheel dug in, you couldn't correct it," Truelove said. "The Mercury that year had five full turns of the steering wheel to make a full turn [of the wheels]. The car started fishtailing until eventually it flipped into the air."

A spectacular sequence of photos of the wreck appeared in *Life* magazine.

Truelove faced a dilemma. His ride home was crumpled.

"There was a fellow who was down there from a dealership in Hartford [Connecticut] who was repossessing Fords," Truelove said. "We took two of the repossessed cars off his hauler and put my car up on top. I drove home in one of the repossessed cars."

It's a Family Thing

If for no other reason than his name, Casey Mears figures to race in the Indianapolis 500 one day.

Mears' uncle, Rick Mears, won the Indy 500 four times (1979, 1984, 1988, and 1991), and his dad, Roger, also competed in the race.

Casey came up through the ranks of open-wheel racing and figured to wind up at its highest levels but detoured to NASCAR. Still, the pull of Indianapolis in May is strong.

Mears saw Indianapolis Motor Speedway for the first time late in 1995 when he traveled to Indianapolis to pick up a United States Auto Club trophy.

"The first time I saw the place was in the snow," he said. "They let me drive around it in a Suburban. It was great. It has a special place in my heart because I've followed it so closely over the years. Even though I didn't go to the races, I watched my uncle. Every time I watch one of his wins now on TV on highlight shows, I get goose bumps. I get excited about it all over again. It gives me the chills."

Drivers Tony Stewart and John Andretti have run both the Indianapolis 500 and NASCAR's Coca-Cola 600 on the same day, and that could be an option for Mears at some point. It would be the fulfillment of a dream.

Rice—Not Booze—in the Infield

What do you do with a racetrack that isn't a racetrack anymore? In at least one case, you grow a bumper crop of rice on it.

That's the situation at the former Memphis-Arkansas Speedway, a 1.5-mile, high-banked dirt track that hosted the NASCAR Cup Series from 1954 to 1957. One of the most dangerous tracks in NASCAR's first decade, the track was purchased by Eubanks Farms, an adjacent farming operation, in 1957 and returned to its former assignment—growing rice.

The 20-degree banked turns of the old track, located in LeHi 14 miles from the Mississippi River off Interstate 40, remain visible, although they now are covered with green vegetation. Rice covers the sprawling infield.

The speedway was too fast for its time. It was built with the idea that it eventually would be paved, but the owners ran out of money after running five NASCAR dirt-track events in four years.

There were two driver deaths and numerous injuries at the track, which, at its opening, was billed as the longest dirt track in the world. It certainly was the longest oval NASCAR drivers had challenged to that point.

"That track was something," said retired driver Cotton Owens. "It was rough, and you got through the turns the best way you could. It had so many holes. It was so dusty you couldn't see."

During the first race, held on October 10, 1954, four drivers and two crewmen were hospitalized. Among them was Jimmy Nichols, a mechanic from Randleman, North Carolina. He was badly burned in a fire in the pits.

In 1955 Tiny Lund, who would go on to become one of NASCAR's most beloved drivers, made his series debut at the track. It almost became his first and last race. He was thrown from his car when it flipped several times on the race's 67th lap. Ralph Liguori was among the drivers in the wake of the wreck, and he hit Lund's helmet.

"We were coming around the third and fourth turns, and he caught a rut or something and flipped," Liguori said. "He came out of the car, and I ran over him. I thought I had killed him. I got word he was alive and conscious. When I went to the hospital to see him that night, he said, 'What happened? I heard you ran over me. How come?' I said, 'Well, I thought you were dead, so I wasn't going to swerve to miss you.'"

Of course, Liguori was kidding. Ironically Lund was sponsored in the race by a safety-belt company, and his belts had failed in the crash.

The track was plagued by rainouts and by relentless dust. According to newspaper reports, most of the crowd of 10,000 in attendance for the final race in 1957 left before the halfway point because dust made the race virtually impossible to see.

Parker Eubanks now farms the track property as part of an operation that totals 11,000 acres.

"If they had had money to asphalt the track, they would have made it," said Eubanks, who saw the speedway's first race as a kid. "I think NASCAR would still be here. Just imagine what a place it could have been."

Stewart Rides the Bus

Because he grew up in Indiana and has a special love for the Indianapolis 500, Tony Stewart always will have a strong connection to Indianapolis Motor Speedway.

Stewart, a winner in the Brickyard 400 at Indy, has been a visitor or competitor in races at the world-famous track since he was a kid.

He was a small child when his father took him to his first Indy 500, but that trip remains fresh in his memory.

"We were in some bus that had a luggage rack in the top of it," he said. "You had to get up [very early] to get on the bus to ride up to Indy for race day.

"They threw me up in the luggage rack. Somebody gave me a pillow, and everybody started throwing their jackets on top of me to keep me warm.

"The ride home wasn't nearly as cool, because after a long day at the track, everybody but my dad and I were kind of rowdy."

When Teammates Aren't Teammates

Racing at Daytona International Speedway and Talladega Superspeedway is a very different animal from the competitions at every other track on the NASCAR circuit.

Because engine-restrictor plates are used at those two tracks, much of the 43-car field typically is bunched in large packs. The plates and the draft are big equalizers, and it's practically impossible for one car to pull away from the others.

In the Daytona/Talladega draft, two or more cars in a line typically perform better than one car alone, and passes often are made with one driver "pushing" another forward into a better position.

It should follow, then, that teammates would be exceptionally valuable in these races. They can hook up and help each other, particularly late in a race when help is needed most.

Oddly, though, the intricacies of the draft make such scenarios difficult to produce. In the heat of the moment, with one or two laps to go, drivers usually fall in line with the car that seems the most likely to benefit them, even if it isn't driven by a teammate.

Although there often is a lot of talk prior to the race about teammates helping teammates (and even some prerace plotting), once the battle begins, the landscape usually changes.

"At the end of the day, if Kevin Harvick helped me finish third and he finished eighth and could have finished fourth, he did the wrong thing," said Jeff Burton, a Harvick teammate at Richard Childress Racing. "That is just how it is. Anybody who thinks teammates go into the race thinking we are going to work with each other all day long is crazy. You don't run with each other all day long. It doesn't happen that way.

"There is a time at some point late in the race when your teammate does something and you can try to help him make sure it helps him. But that is a very situational thing, and we have a rule that if you can help me without hurting yourself, do it, but if you are going to hurt yourself, I don't want you to do it. That is not fair to you, your team, your sponsor, and everybody involved.

"We work together, but we don't go into the race thinking that. If you do think that every time you do something your teammate is going to go with you, you are destined to be mad. That is just how it is.

"We are selfish, self-centered, arrogant people. That is how we are supposed to be. It is not about helping other people; it is about doing what you need to do for yourself. That is what competition is. You can't live your life like that, but if you aren't willing to race like that, you won't be successful."

Yarborough Flips One

One of the most dramatic crashes in Daytona International Speedway history occurred with only one car—Cale Yarborough's orange-and-white Chevrolet—on the track.

During qualifying for the 1983 Daytona 500, Yarborough turned a speed of 200.503 mph—then a record—on his first time-trial lap. He was surging toward an even faster speed on his second lap when his car suddenly turned sideways in the third turn, lifted into the air, and slammed down on its roof.

Yarborough wasn't hurt, but the car was mangled, and his Ranier Racing team went to a backup car for the 500.

The story has a happy ending. Yarborough won the 500, his third victory in the race.

Indy and Daytona Meet at Top

When Indianapolis Motor Speedway joined the NASCAR Cup circuit in 1994, there were questions about how longtime Indy fans would accept stock cars and how the general auto-racing population would support the Brickyard 400 in terms of ticket sales.

The answers came quickly. Virtually everything was positive. Although there was some grumbling by Indy traditionalists, fans responded at the ticket booths with exuberance, swarming over the world's most famous speedway.

The NASCAR stop at Indy drew such crowds and interest that discussions began almost immediately about its position in the sport versus other top races. The Daytona 500 has been considered NASCAR's No. 1 event since its first running in 1959, and its trophy always has been the most coveted by most drivers. A win at Indianapolis is a treasure, too, however.

Jimmie Johnson and Jeff Gordon have won both.

"I am asked the question often, and it is so hard to answer it because they both have a certain feeling that just kind of fulfills inside of me," Johnson said. "I can say that [with] my little trophy case, the way that things line up is that I have my Nextel Cup championship trophy as the centerpiece, and then on either side of it is the Daytona 500 trophy and the Brickyard trophy.

"They are very, very similar, and I think for the history of our sport, Daytona has a little bit more to it, but Indy is right there, if not on a par with it."

Gordon, who has multiple wins in both races, said the Daytona 500 clearly is NASCAR's biggest event but that his biggest win was scored in the first Brickyard 400.

"I don't know how other people rank it, but it's the one that stands out in my mind," he said. "I want to win the Daytona 500, but there is just a little something in the back of your mind when you come to Indy and you think, man, I really, really want this one.

"The other thing is that a restrictor-plate race at Daytona takes a little bit away from your chances. It makes it sort of not that anybody can win it, but a lot more guys can win it. Here [at Indianapolis], the driver plays a really big role."

New Boots for A.J.

Atlanta Motor Speedway has struggled with weather issues over the years, with rain a frequent race-week visitor to the track in sub-urban Hampton, Georgia.

NASCAR President Mike Helton is very acquainted with that situation. He was first public-relations director and later general manager of the track.

Rain during a race weekend in the early 1980s cost the track's front office a few extra dollars—for a pair of cowboy boots.

"Walt Nix owned the track then, and he was a big A.J. Foyt fan," Helton said. "He always liked it when A.J. would come there and race. It rained a lot during a race weekend once, and one of our drivers' parking lots was behind the old garage area. A.J. stepped out of his car and goes down into mud about to his knees. When his feet came up out of the hole, he didn't have his boots on.

"So we ended up replacing a pair of pretty high-end Texas cowboy boots."

chapter 9
Characters, Inc.

Dick Brooks was a true NASCAR character. Brought up in logging camps and tent villages, he began racing as an independent in 1970. Though he never became a superstar, he was successful enough to support himself comfortably, and he had great respect from the racing community.

Perhaps the very nature of NASCAR
racing attracts those who live in a parallel
universe on the very edges of life.

Over the years, more than a few true characters
have rolled through the sport. Some have been
eccentric, some wild, some both.

He Was Still Waiting for a Train

Dick Brooks was a racing original.

Brooks, who died in 2006, was raised in logging camps in the Pacific Northwest. His father followed the availability of logging work from place to place, and Brooks spent much of his youth living in tent villages. It was an unusual, disconnected childhood, but it also was one of great adventure—both real and imagined. In Brooks' make-believe world, he could be almost anyone he wanted to be.

On Sunday afternoons in those camps, Brooks discovered stock-car racing in an unlikely way. He first heard the roar of stock-car thunder on the radio.

A big, battery-powered (necessary because of the camps' remote locations) radio unit put the young Brooks in Darlington, South Carolina, and elsewhere on the NASCAR circuit, and the men racing on those far-flung, mysterious tracks became his heroes.

"We could listen to the radio only once or twice a week, because the battery would run down," Brooks said. "I strung a wire through the trees in the mountains to get reception for the races. I did whatever it took to listen to them."

He got his chance to join them in 1969, beginning a long career as a driver by racing in the first event he ever saw—the Daytona 500. Brooks wound up in that great middle swath of journeyman racers who enjoy a win or two but generally scramble for good rides and high finishes. Much of his success came while he was driving for another stock-car original—Virginia car owner Junie Donlavey. Donlavey seldom had the money to try to run up front, but he was greatly respected all along pit road as one of the game's great gentlemen.

"I never dreamed that I could be in the racing world," Brooks said. "It certainly wasn't planned. I doubt if I was even planned, and none of the rest of my life has been, either. Planning all this stuff out would be out of character for me."

Brooks, who made enough money to live comfortably and own a string of automobile dealerships, perhaps gained his greatest popularity in the aftermath of his driving career when he joined Motor Racing Network's radio team as a pit reporter, ironically returning to the place where he had been introduced to the sport. He roamed the garages of speedways in bib overalls—the more pockets to carry his stuff, he reasoned—and interviewed drivers and crew chiefs about the business of the day.

Beyond the track, Brooks was a hoot. His hobbies leaned toward fast and expensive vehicles—two-wheel, four-wheel, and airborne. He once tipped over a small airplane while taxiing on the runway of his farm near Spartanburg, South Carolina. Afterward, he told friends that, with the airplane incident, he had crashed everything except a train.

Brooks' most serious accident occurred on a motorcycle. In July 1999 he crashed his bike on a South Carolina country road, sustained serious injuries, and kept friends in a worried state about his recovery for months. Fellow retired driver and friend David Pearson visited Brooks in the hospital after the accident. Brooks, banged up and woozy, told Pearson that his attending doctor was optimistic that he eventually would "get back to about 80 percent of [him]self."

"Hell, Brooks," Pearson said, "that's better than you were before."

City Meets Country in "Last American Hero" Saga

Writer Tom Wolfe lives in the heart of New York City, wears shockingly white expensive suits, and dines with the elite of Manhattan. NASCAR icon Junior Johnson lives on the edge of the North Carolina mountains, wears overalls or jeans, and dines on bacon and ham at early-morning breakfasts with the boys.

Yet Wolfe and Johnson are fast friends. They became so in the 1960s when Wolfe, then working for *Esquire* magazine, decided to do a story on the rise of stock-car racing and how the automobile had become such a symbol of the surging South.

That article was "The Last American Hero Is Junior Johnson. Yes!" It appeared in the March 1965 issue of *Esquire* and remains one of the most widely praised pieces of sports journalism ever published. Wolfe masterfully weaved the story of Johnson, a rough-hewn mountain boy–turned–racing king, and the automobile-happy South into a brilliant overview of one time and one place.

Wolfe arrived in the foothills of the North Carolina mountains in the spring of 1964 to begin work on the story. Still dressed in his New York finery, he met Johnson at a small country store, talked to him briefly, and found himself returning to the area several times as he gathered material for his story.

"I became really interested not only in stock-car racing, but in Junior himself and the way the South had changed," said Wolfe, who grew up in Richmond, Virginia. "In most peoples' minds—in mine, really, although I grew up in the South—the South was still Erskine Caldwell's South from the 1930s.

"But, by this time, it had changed so much. Automobiles changed so many things. It became a real culture—exciting. New York, for example, is the only place in the country where you run into people who can't drive. Adults who can't drive. They've never had to depend on cars. A lot about New York is decades old. You do more walking here than any place I know of in the country."

Wolfe became fascinated with Johnson and his background.

"Junior was, in a way, very, very reserved," he said. "He's not the kind of person who's going to go on and on for his autobiography. He's just not going to do it. He's not holding back on you. It's just embarrassing to talk that much about yourself. That was the impression I got, but there were lots of other people who had idolized him and had Junior Johnson stories. He was—well, *mythic* is too fancy a word, but, *icon*, let's put it that way."

Managing the Marigolds with Jimmy

Jimmy Spencer, the big, bruising race-car driver who has been known to throw a punch or two, is a gardener.

Yes, it's true.

Spencer spends some of his spare time working in his yard and urging the perennials along.

"A lot of people can't believe it," Spencer said. "But I think deep down inside, everybody would like to have a nice yard. There's nothing better than to go out in your yard and sit in the grass and talk to your kids.

"I grew up in a junkyard. My mom always wanted to have a really nice yard. I ride around now and look at new houses and how they're decorating them and how they're doing the yards. Then I saw all this stuff in the garden shops, and I started asking questions. It's fun. I don't get to spend enough time there."

Although some people see yard work as exactly that—work—Spencer said it's pleasant time off for him.

"It sounds like a lot of work, but it's not work at all," he said. "It's relaxation. It's digging down and getting dirty. I love it when I see the earthworms, because I know I've got good, healthy soil."

You can take a good thing too far, though, he learned.

"An old guy told me, yeah, chicken manure is the best fertilizer in the world. He told me to put a little, not a lot, on my plants, but I figured if a little bit is good, I'll put a lot on. I killed me a bunch of plants, just murdered them."

Yates Goes out on a Limb for Johnson

Robert Yates, a successful team owner and the son of a preacher, will go down in NASCAR history as one of the sport's greatest engine builders.

Yates got much of his education at Holman-Moody (H-M), the now-defunct auto-racing giant that fueled the careers of many in NASCAR. He joined H-M in 1968 and scored his first engine-built victory in 1969 when LeeRoy Yarbrough drove Junior Johnson's Ford to a win in the Daytona 500.

The story behind that win is a bit unusual.

"All the Ford teams had gone to Riverside [speedway in California] in 1969, and just about every team had broken rod bolts," Yates remembered. "The supplier had changed the rod bolts and exchanged all of the existing bolts at Holman-Moody for the new bolts. Before they took the old bolts, I held back one set.... When so many broke at Riverside, I felt it was just a bad run of bolts.

"So all the guys were on their way to Daytona Beach. Junior Johnson came to me, and he agreed with me that the rod bolts were the problem. Management said that everybody got the new rod bolts, with no exceptions. Management supported the supplier that said the bolts were not the problem. Junior wanted the old bolts, and I told him I had a set. If I'd had enough, I'd have done it for every team. I only had one set and only one guy wanting them.

"I stuck my neck out. Junior asked just to put the bolts in the engines already at Daytona. But our people would never have allowed that. I told him I could put an engine together and would put the old bolts in. He said, 'We've got to have it tomorrow.' I said I could do it and put in an all-nighter and got an engine together and had it 'dynoed' out the next morning by 7:00.

"Junior went to Daytona, and that's the engine that was in Junior's car when LeeRoy Yarbrough won the race. I was sweating my job over that deal. When they ran the race, I was in Charlotte in my mother-in-law's backyard with a rake. I don't know how much raking I was doing, but I was sure swinging that rake a lot listening to the race on the radio."

Aunt Noreen Taught Him the Ropes

Larry McReynolds, now one of the most popular broadcasters in NASCAR racing, got involved in motorsports because of his Aunt Noreen.

Noreen Mears ran hobby-division races at tracks in and around Birmingham, Alabama, McReynolds' hometown. He started hanging around those races, performing various duties and catching a permanent case of the racing bug.

From those humble beginnings as a kid, McReynolds advanced from short-track racing to crew-chief positions on top NASCAR teams to a prominent analyst's spot in racing television.

His first big step, after Aunt Noreen, came with a shot-in-the-dark phone call.

McReynolds was working during the day at a salvage yard and during the night on race cars owned by Birmingham car builder Bobby Ray Jones. The long hours and the desire to race full-time prompted him to go job hunting, and a classified ad in a NASCAR publication in the summer of 1980 caught his eye.

Greenville, South Carolina, businessman Bob Rogers was putting together a Cup team and was looking for mechanics. McReynolds responded to the ad by telephone and was working with Rogers' small operation a few weeks later.

Eight years later, working with drag racer Kenny Bernstein's King Racing Cup team, McReynolds got his first Cup victory with driver Ricky Rudd.

"I'll always be thankful that Bob Rogers and his family had enough faith in this voice they were talking to on the other end of the phone to hire him," McReynolds said.

Johnson Endorses Mule Power

Junior Johnson grew up on a farm and learned the ins and outs of making things grow before he detoured into a career in auto racing.

The simple things—like plowing with a mule—still ring true for him, despite his prominence and wealth.

"If you're going to have a garden, you better have a mule," Johnson said. "You can have a tractor, but you ain't going to have as good a garden. Besides, they're a lot of fun if you want to just, you know, mess with them.

"Some people ride them back through the hills and stuff like that, but I basically just use one to tend my garden with. I plowed one out when I was a young kid, so, you know, it's sort of a traditional thing with me. When I'm going to plant a garden, it's fun to plow it with a mule. Raising a garden with a tractor don't intrigue me like a mule does."

It's a different form of horsepower.

Johnson Ready to "Help You'ns"

Junior Johnson is all about getting things straight and keeping things straight. Throughout his racing career, he was a straight shooter with news media, drivers, officials, and others who crossed his considerable path. When rumors began spreading about his racing team, he was quick to set the record right.

So it was that Johnson, irritated about newspaper reports about the possibility that he might sell his team, opened an April 17, 1993, press conference at North Wilkesboro Speedway with this statement:

"Guys, basically what I want to do is kind of answer some of you people's questions. I read stuff in the paper, and you're writing stuff that's not exactly what has went on in my situation of racing. Plus, Mike [newspaper reporter Mike Mulhern] put out an article that said the teams were for sale and that kind of stuff. I want to answer them kind of questions and any other questions that you have and stop some of the gossip that's not true.

"I want to help you'ns get the answers you want without somebody giving them to you that don't know what the hell's happened. Any of the questions I can answer, that's what I want to do. There ain't no sense in stuff being written that's not true, and some of the things that's said is just fantasy stuff. Some of you'ns I've already talked to and set you straight on some of these things that's happening in our operation, and some of you'ns I haven't. So anything I can answer for you, feel free to ask me whatever you'ns want to about anything you've got on your mind."

It was classic Junior.

A Very Fast Senior Citizen

James Hylton, who started racing NASCAR Cup cars in 1964, made a remarkable attempt to return to the sport in 2007 by trying to qualify for the Daytona 500 at the age of 72.

And he almost made it.

Hylton attracted a flood of media attention by going up against drivers two generations removed. There was a lot of kidding—for example, if he made the race, would he stop for diaper changes?—and Hylton endured all of it gracefully.

"I'm just happy to be here," he said. "I think I can still do this. You don't forget how to race."

Hylton finished a few positions too low in a 150-mile qualifying race and didn't make the 500 field. He was disappointed but was pleased with the effort in an underfunded car and vowed to race again.

Hylton raced with minor sponsorship for most of his 30-year driving career but finished second to champion David Pearson in the 1966 point race and won two races—at Richmond in 1970 and at Talladega, Alabama, in 1972.

How to Lose Your Fingers

Driver and television commentator Wally Dallenbach Jr. spends much of his time at racetracks amid the noise, crowds, and general busyness of auto racing. To occasionally get away from that, Dallenbach goes to extremes—other continents, for example.

Dallenbach is a big-game hunter and has traveled to many corners of the Earth in pursuit of prey. He has hunted lions and elephants in Africa, alligators in the swamps of Florida, and bears in Alaska. One of those Alaska trips was particularly memorable.

"A brown-bear hunt I was on in Alaska was probably the most memorable because he charged me," Dallenbach said. "I've

James Hylton watches qualifying runs for the Daytona 500 on February 11, 2007. Hylton, who raced NASCAR Cup cars in the 1960s and 1970s, made an attempt to return to the sport by trying to qualify for the 2007 Daytona 500 at 72 years of age.

hunted all my life, and you hear stories about charges, and I'd never had anything charge me. It was pretty exciting.

"I'd been to Alaska three or four times and never even seen a bear, let alone one this size. He was a monster, 10 and a half feet tall. We found a moose kill, and we knew he was in the area by a big set of tracks. We decided we'd wait for him.

"About four hours later, we saw him headed in there. We went in after him, and we knew we'd either scare him off or he'd be on top of us. We walked out in this little clearing and stopped. All of a sudden, it sounded like a train was coming. We could hear him running and woofing. He came blowing out of that clearing.

"When he saw us, he got up on his hind legs and started walking toward us. That's when I decided he had gotten close enough. I shot him probably 12 paces from where I stood. It was a very impressive animal. I've gotten some black bears, and black bears are sissies compared to these animals."

In the summer of 1999 Dallenbach shot a 12-foot alligator on a hunt through the Florida swamplands. The kill raised an interesting question: after you shoot a 700-pound alligator, how do you move it from deep in a swamp to civilization?

"You have to get them before they sink [in the river]," Dallenbach said. "Normally, I'm not the first one to jump into the water and start that process. One time we got one that did sink. There's a guy who lives near Bunnell, Florida, nicknamed Cowboy. He went into that creek and started diving for it, trying to touch the bottom and feel the gator.

"Cowboy's only got about four fingers. You'll know him when you see him. I guess it's kind of everyday stuff for him, because he grew up around it.

"For me, I'd never seen anybody dive for a gator. It was pretty cool. Then you put them on a boat—when the boat's 10 feet and the gator is 12, it can get interesting—and haul them out. Or sometimes you have to drag them through the woods. It helps to have a four-wheeler."

That's Geoffrey, Please

Between the 1998 and 1999 racing seasons, driver Geoff Bodine suddenly became driver Geoffrey Bodine.

It isn't often that a driver chooses to change the name he officially uses for race entry forms and NASCAR results, but Bodine, a veteran racer, did just that.

"Geoffrey is my real name," he said at the time. "My mother named me that when I was born and spelled it with a G. I guess she did that to be different. It cursed me for a while when I was in high school. I got called a lot of names because of the spelling.

"When I got into Winston Cup, I believe I was the only Geoff. It stayed that way for quite a while. Now we have three or four others. You have a lot of Mikes and Joes and Petes and all that and Dales. I like to be different.

"Walking down pit road and in the garage, the fans call out your name. If you're walking with Gordon or Burton or Green [all Jeffs], everybody turned around, and you really didn't know who they wanted. Of course, you knew if you were with Gordon it was really him. I've got to start winning some races so it'll be me.

"I've got a different spelling, and if I use the full name, well, if somebody says 'Jeff' now, I don't even look. If they say 'Geoffrey,' I turn around, and I know it's me."

Martin Rapping Along

Who knew? Mark Martin is a fan of rap music.

It might take a while to digest that fact.

Yes, Martin, one of the most popular racers in NASCAR history and one of the most accomplished professional sports figures to emerge from the state of Arkansas, has quite a rap collection.

His favorite? Prepare for this: Eminem.

"Eminem is probably the one that got me hooked originally quite a few years ago," Martin said.

All this started years before the 2006 release of a rap anthem honoring Martin. Titled "Start Your Engines," the song is performed by Budda Early.

"Man, I love it," Martin said. "I think they did a great job. I know that some of you think it's kind of funny. My wife, Arlene, and Matt [his son] tell me I'm too old to listen to rap. A lot of people are surprised that I like rap and hip-hop. A lot of people are surprised, including my own family, when they catch me listening to country."

Martin said the storylines in rap music attracted him to the songs.

Montoya Leaves Monaco for Darlington

Juan Pablo Montoya seemed out of place when he jumped into NASCAR racing in 2006. A native of Colombia, Montoya had raced Indy cars and had been a sensation on the international Formula One circuit. Now he wanted to try stock cars, and an old friend, team owner Chip Ganassi, gave him that chance.

It was quite a shock to the NASCAR world, one mostly made up of Americans brought up on oval-track racing.

"Anybody who will try that has a lot of confidence in their ability," said NASCAR driver John Andretti, who also had raced on other circuits. "He didn't have to make this move. He still had opportunities in Formula One. This is like going into a jungle when you've never been in one before. It takes a pretty confident and brave person to do that.

"If you're off 0.3 of a second in NASCAR, you're junk. If you're off 0.3 of a second in Formula One, you're third on the grid."

Montoya eased into NASCAR with some test runs and competition in ARCA, then ran the full Cup circuit and a partial Busch schedule in 2007. He surprised many by scoring wins in both Cup and Busch in '07. He also carried his reputation for aggressive driving from Formula One into NASCAR, which ruffled feathers here and there.

"For me, I'm here for the long run, whether they like it or not," Montoya said. "Do I want to succeed? Of course, I want to succeed. Is it going to be easy? No. Am I going to have bad races? Definitely, yes. It's part of it."

He made some adjustments rapidly and others not so quickly. By midseason, though, it was clear that he was ready to make noise. And people heard him.

Most drivers in the garage area accepted Montoya quickly. Jeff Burton spoke for many when he said Montoya's arrival was big, for more than one reason.

"I wish we were at a place in our society where we didn't have to talk about Juan Montoya because he's not from here," Burton said. "It's sad that we're not there. It's not a NASCAR issue. It's a society issue. At some point, we've got to get past that. And I'll be damn glad when we do.

"The thing that interests me more about Montoya than him being Hispanic or anything else that has anything to do with that is that I think through this we have a great opportunity for NASCAR fans to understand that there are great drivers that don't drive stock cars. And I think we also have a great opportunity for F1 fans to understand that this is really hard. And that we're not just a bunch of dumb, unintelligent rednecks with cherry pickers taking engines out of trees. I think those groups of fans are going to have a much better appreciation for what the others do."

A Tick in Time

Tom Giacchi never expected the situation to get so hairy.

In November 2005 Giacchi, Carl Edwards' motor-coach driver, decided he wouldn't shave his beard until Edwards won another race. He had no idea at that point, of course, that Edwards would go winless in 2006. The beard grew and grew and grew.

It got so long that creatures started moving in.

"He probably won't like me telling this story," Edwards said, "but yesterday he's sitting there in the motor home with my trainer and I, and Tom goes, 'Man, I think I've got a tick here in my beard.'

"I said, 'No, dude. No way. That's nasty.'"

In June 2007 Edwards finally produced relief for Giacchi. Edwards won the Cup race at Michigan, ending a 52-race winless string, and allowing his Yeti-like motor-coach driver to shave.

By that time, Giacchi had built up something of a cult following and even had his own website. He was more than ready to end the drama, however. The beard was gone shortly after Edwards' win.

chapter 10

The Times Were Golden

Junior Johnson poses next to his No. 11 Ford before a 1958 race in Columbia, South Carolina. In 1958 Johnson returned to racing after serving parts of 1956 and 1957 in prison for a bootleg-whiskey charge.

Chainsaws? Cooked tires? A ham in victory lane?

NASCAR's formative years saw some weird and strange stuff. The sport was trying to invent itself, and it was quite natural that things were occasionally a little off-balance.

Here's Tobacco in Your Ear

Joe Epton was NASCAR's first chief scorer. In the sport's pioneer days, that was a job that didn't involve much technology. Basically, Epton had a pencil, some paper, and an assistant.

As the cars passed the start/finish line every lap, Harry Sink, Epton's helper, would yell the numbers to Epton, in order, and Epton would write them on a pad. It wasn't sensationally scientific, but it usually worked, and it was NASCAR's basic way of scoring for many years.

"It was just the two of us scoring the races in the early days," Epton said. "Harry yelled the numbers in my ear. He smoked cigars. It took me three days to get the tobacco out of my ear.

"But that's all it was—me and a pencil and Harry Sink."

NASCAR scoring is now handled by an elaborate computer system that can spit out speeds, positions, and differences in car-positioning in fractions of a second.

It's more efficient, but it may not be as much fun.

A Chainsaw? That Got Their Attention

The first race in what became the NASCAR Cup Series was held on June 19, 1949, at the now-defunct Charlotte Speedway, a .75-mile dirt track in Charlotte, North Carolina.

Promoter Bill France Sr. might have been concerned about how the public would accept this new thing. Not to worry.

"There were fans here at six AM that day," said David Allison, whose father, Carl, owned the track. David, then a child, worked that first race.

"They came from everywhere. Cars were parked as far as four miles away. People were trying to get in everywhere. We had people climbing trees to see. Daddy would crank up a chainsaw and go over there. He wouldn't actually cut the trees down, but they would come out of them anyway."

The actual crowd total that day probably will never be known. Estimates have ranged from 12,000 to 23,000 people. What those spectators saw was a ragged 200-lap race between "showroom stock" cars with very few modifications. Among those competing were men who would be the foundation of future Halls of Fame—Curtis Turner, Buck Baker, Lee Petty, Herb Thomas, Red Byron, Tim Flock, Jack Smith, and others.

Among the spectators was Ned Jarrett, who later would race into Hall of Fame status himself. "I was standing next to the fence at the start/finish line," Jarrett said. "I thought that was the place to be. All of a sudden, a car came down through there, and a fan blade flew off and stuck in the wooden post right where I was leaning. I quickly figured out that was not the place to be."

At the end of a long afternoon, Glenn Dunnaway of Gastonia, North Carolina, emerged as the race winner. But his 1947 Ford, a converted moonshine-hauler, was ruled illegal because the car's rear end had been strengthened to support heavy loads of liquor.

Second-place Jim Roper, who had traveled from Kansas for the race, was awarded the victory. He had driven his 1949 Lincoln from Kansas, picked up the race win, and then drove the car home. He never won again.

The Charlotte track was closed in 1956 because the land was needed to build a section of interstate highway. It is several miles from the current Lowe's Motor Speedway in Concord, North Carolina.

Up, Up, and Away

After three years without a victory, Junior Johnson returned to NASCAR's win list May 18, 1958, by winning a 100-mile race at North Wilkesboro (North Carolina) Speedway, his home track.

There were a couple of backstories attached to the victory. It was Johnson's first win since he had been released from prison after serving parts of 1956 and 1957 for involvement in the illegal whiskey business in the North Carolina mountains.

Also, the win came despite the fact that Johnson actually drove his race car out of the track during the 160-lap event.

Leading late in the race, Johnson sailed into the third turn too hard and went over the track banking.

"I turned it around on the outside of the racetrack, just spun it around, and it was real high-banked coming back in, so I knew if I didn't come back in real fast, I'd get hung up as I came over the bank there," Johnson said. "So I just mashed it wide open, and I came back toward the racetrack wide open, and that thing went over the top of it. I was about a half-lap ahead when I went over it, and when I came back on the racetrack I was about a half-lap behind."

Johnson beat Jack Smith to the finish line by six seconds.

Since Johnson grew up not too far from the track in Ronda, North Carolina, he was one of North Wilkesboro's great racing heroes. His performance that day perhaps sealed that position.

Thomas: From Tractor to Race Car

Herb Thomas might be called NASCAR's first superstar. And he was an accidental one, at that.

Thomas was a farmer at heart. He raised corn and tobacco in North Carolina and stumbled into racing mostly by accident. He attended a Modified race in Greensboro in the late 1940s. The action got his attention, and he quickly decided that he could do as well as the drivers in the race.

"I went to Greensboro to see a race and figured if they could do it, I could, too," Thomas said. "It was something I liked to do. I got to beat somebody else."

Thomas entered the first Cup (then Strictly Stock) race in Charlotte in 1949 and soon showed his skills. He became the series' first two-time champion (in 1951 and 1953) and also was the first driver to win the storied Southern 500, one of NASCAR's most difficult races, three times (in 1951, 1954, and 1955).

Thomas raced in the sport's formative years, when drivers often drove their race cars to the track, competed, and then drove the car home. "I remember playing the radio in a race car," he said.

"I raced at a track up in New York where the dust was so thick, all you could see was the tops of trees at each end of the track. You looked for the trees, then turned. Then you'd go to the other end, look for the trees, and make a turn."

Thomas' career ended in 1962. He won 48 times. He was among the charter group of five pioneers inducted into the National Motorsports Press Association Hall of Fame in 1965.

After his racing career ended, Thomas returned to farming and also operated a trucking company.

France Jr. Started at the Bottom—of the Fence

Bill France Jr., son of NASCAR's founder, ran the organization for three decades and was front and center for most of the crucial decisions that turned stock-car racing into a national phenomenon.

He started his involvement with a less-than-thrilling assignment. On the day of the first Cup race—June 19, 1949, at Charlotte, North Carolina—France's job was to catch freeloaders who were trying to watch the event without paying. France was 16 years old.

"I remember being on the outside of the fence," he said. "My job was to pull people off the fence who were trying to sneak in or see over. It was a solid wooden fence seven or eight feet high. I'd go up and grab them around the knees and pull them down. Then I'd go about 10 feet and pull another guy down. They'd start to take a swing at me, and I'd run."

Things got a little easier from there, although Bill Jr. would have many other worker-bee jobs at races, including selling programs and snow cones, before he worked his way to the top. He later said all those experiences were valuable and gave him ground-level insight as he dealt with tough decisions on a daily basis.

Yunick Knew His Tires

Smokey Yunick was one of NASCAR's legendary mechanics and innovators.

He feuded with the ruling France family for much of his life, yet he won races and retained a reputation as a man who knew more about the mechanical and technical ends of racing than virtually anybody in the history of motorsports. He crossed the divide between stock-car racing and Indy-car racing and excelled at both.

Smokey Yunick was as unpredictable as his cars. Always looking to implement into his equipment what the rule book didn't say, he kept inspectors—and opponents—on their toes.

Yunick, owner of the self-proclaimed "Best Damn Garage in Town" in Daytona Beach, Florida, took many of his technical secrets to the grave with him, but some seeped out over the years.

"In 1955 Smokey went up to Firestone in Akron [Ohio] and wanted to go through the junk pile," remembered Humpy Wheeler, a wildly successful track promoter and executive for most of his career, but once Firestone's representative in racing. "Firestone always had a pile of tires that had been tried somewhere and didn't work. Smokey picked out four Indy-car tires that were harder compound, that were being discarded because they just were too hard.

"That's what he put on the '55 Chevrolet that Herb Thomas won the Southern 500 in [at Darlington Raceway]. Went 500 miles without a tire change."

It was just another race day that Yunick dominated with his thinking cap.

Hey, Don't Overcook That Goodyear

Tires in an oven?

NASCAR competitors have gone in many unusual directions over the years in attempts to gain a technological edge, but roasting tires admittedly was rather strange.

Jack Smith, one of stock-car racing's pioneer drivers, remembered tinkering of that sort going on with regularity.

"People found out they could take tires, put them out in the sun, put them in an oven, soften the tires, and put them on the left side or get a tire recapping company to do it," Smith said. "At the Peach Bowl Speedway in Atlanta, I found out that Jones Tire Company was a recapping company. I could get him to recap the tires for the left side and put a certain compound and heat it to a certain temperature.

"It was just like day-and-night difference in how it handled. People always accused me of cheating on the motors. We didn't have to cheat on the motors. All we had to do was get the car to handling. Any way you could get tires heated to a certain temperature and then bring them out and cool them off, that made a difference.

"You could even use a kitchen-type oven."

Make mine well done, please.

Racing a Ragtop

In-car cameras have given television viewers new and unique looks at what drivers experience during races, but the ability to see inside competing race cars isn't entirely new.

Grandstand fans could watch drivers battle each other—and the track—when NASCAR raced convertibles for several years in the late 1950s. The sport's Convertible Division lasted from 1956 to 1959, but the ragtops lingered at some tracks, notably Darlington Raceway, where they were quite popular. The last convertible race was held in 1963.

The first superspeedway race for convertibles was held at Darlington in 1957. Fireball Roberts was the winner.

"One of the things people really liked about the convertibles was that at most racetracks they could see you plain as day in there," said driver Jack Smith, who raced in that first Darlington event. "They could see you work your hands and react to everything. A lot of people liked them better than the hardtops."

For the drivers, Smith said, the racing was much the same as in standard cars. "They went at it just like normal, but they really mixed it up," he said. "Joe Weatherly, Curtis Turner, Larry Frank, Bob Welborn, all those guys. They had some real shows in those convertibles."

Drivers raced in actual factory convertibles or in regular Grand National cars that had had their hardtops temporarily removed. The cars could be "convertibles" one week and sedans the next.

"We would put the top back on and bolt it down, and it was no problem," Smith said. "It did create a funny problem for us one time, though. We had run Darlington in a '59 Chevy with the top cut off. Then we took the car to Daytona. We had drilled some holes in the car right above the windshield. I'd go out in practice and come in and tell the crew the rear end was tearing up. That's the way it sounded. But we'd change gears, everything, and it didn't make any difference. Finally, I put a finger over the holes, and that stopped the noise. That fixed it."

In addition to the Convertible Division races, the hardtops and ragtops raced together in some events.

"We could really whip the hardtops on the short tracks," said Larry Frank. "But the superspeedways were different. The hardtops were probably six or eight miles-per-hour faster at Daytona. There would be a pack of four to six of us in convertibles, and a bunch of hardtops would go by, and they'd turn your car right or left, depending on where they were. It really made the steering wheel a handful.

"But it was really good for the fans, especially at a place like Darlington. They could see what you were doing. And I think the drivers liked it, too. It was so much better in an open car. You could see the crowd. There was less noise in the car because it was so much more wide-open, and you could pick up more crowd noise. There was a much freer feeling."

Wanna Race? Wanna Fight?

James "Buck" Clardy was one of those guys who was around at the creation. He raced stock cars from the mid-1940s to 1955 (when a highway accident ended his career) and battled against some of the kings of the pioneer days of the sport.

Clardy said he tangled with Curtis Turner, regarded by many as the best dirt-track racer of all time and a no-holds-barred driver who would punch your car in the rear and you in the face.

"Turner was hard-headed," said Clardy, a South Carolina resident. "I went up to Charlotte to run on the old three-quarter-mile dirt track up there, and of all the people to pick on, I picked on Curtis Turner. He and I hooked up, and I spun him out. I was wild

Curtis Turner was a hard-headed, quick-fisted racer who was around from the dawning of stock-car racing.

as a rabbit. It was the first time I'd ever seen him. He was mad, and I was, too. He pushed me, and I pushed him.

"We got over it, years later."

That kind of interaction between drivers wasn't unusual in the early days, Clardy said.

"You kind of made up the rules as you went, back then," he said. "I've seen 26 drivers fighting in the infield at Greenwood [South Carolina] at one time, and 24 of them didn't know what they were fighting for."

A Southern Sport? Not Exactly

Although NASCAR racing was viewed for much of its history as a Southern sport, its early organizers didn't see it in that mold.

Evidence? There were eight races scheduled in the first season of Cup racing (then known as Strictly Stock) in 1949. Two of the eight were held in Pennsylvania, and one was held in New York.

For a Southern sport, it seems odd that almost half of the first season's races were held outside that region.

Langhorne Speedway, a one-mile dirt track, and Heidelberg Raceway in Pittsburgh, a half-mile dirt track, hosted the Pennsylvania races, with Curtis Turner and Lee Petty scoring the wins, respectively.

Jack White won the other race, at the half-mile Hamburg Speedway in Hamburg, New York.

Race Hard—but Be Careful

Although modern NASCAR teams operate with dozens of race cars, stock-car drivers tried to make ends meet in the 1940s and 1950s with one car, sometimes two.

The late Jack Smith, one of stock-car racing's pioneer drivers and a 21-time winner in the Cup Series, remembered racing seven or eight times a week—in the same car.

"I'd race at the Peach Bowl in Atlanta on Sunday, then go to somewhere like Vidalia, Georgia, on Monday, back to the Peach Bowl on Wednesday, to Greenwood, South Carolina, Thursday, and then to whichever tracks were paying the most on Fridays and Saturdays," Smith said.

"I used the same car because I only had one car. I just straightened out the front axle and maybe put a new rear end under it. You knew you had to finish the race and the one the next night or you weren't going to eat good that week."

Did that mean you had to drive carefully? Not according to Smith.

"I never worried about finishing," he said. "The last race I ran, I ran as hard as I'd ever run."

Tim Flock, another of NASCAR's early racers, confirmed that view.

"It was dog-eat-dog back then," he said. "They dropped them flags back then, and we weren't worried about no points. We were worried about making enough money to take home to feed the kids."

First Prize? It's a Ham!

In racing's early years, drivers often didn't know exactly what they were racing for or, indeed, if there would be anything at all for them at the finish line.

Some of racing's first promoters weren't exactly the best corporate citizens. They often ran away with the purse, and the drivers were left empty-handed.

"Any place you raced in the old days, you always kept an eye on the promoter, because he might take off on you," said Sam Packard, a 1940s-era racer and a participant in the 1947 Daytona Beach, Florida, meeting at which NASCAR was founded. "The promoters had been taking off with the money and leaving us stranded and so forth."

Even on good days, the prize for winning wasn't always spectacular, as remembered by pioneer racer Buck Baker.

"I raced once and got a ham and a fifth of wine," he said. "I thought it was a fifth of liquor, and I bought chasers and later found out it was wine."

That was at a short track in South Carolina in the 1940s, Baker said.

Still, he said, he would have raced for nothing.

"I loved to drive fast, and I had a place to do it," he said. "That was my thing. The driving was more fun than the competition to me. It didn't make a lot of difference to me where I finished or who won the race, as long as I got to run.

"It was tough all the way around then. I used to tell the guys in the pits we'd race for 30 minutes and fight for an hour. Driving the cars back then was like having two mad bulls with one set of harness on them. You didn't know where it was going. You mashed the pedal to the floor and went. You just turned it and hoped it turned left until somebody won."

Baker said the steering wheel broke on his car in a race at the Charlotte, North Carolina, fairgrounds track in the 1950s. He picked up a pair of vise grips in the car and used them to guide the car the rest of the way.

"It didn't go as fast as normal, but I finished the race," he said. "I thought it was dangerous, but I didn't pay much attention to it."

Daytona Tested Pioneers

Lester Hunter was an engine builder in the formative years of NASCAR racing. Also a top mechanic in those days, he built winning race cars for Hall of Fame drivers like Cotton Owens, Speedy Thompson, Buck Baker, Jim Paschal, and Joe Weatherly.

Hunter's cars won races on the old Daytona beach-road course with Owens and Thompson behind the wheel in the mid-1950s. When the beach course closed and Daytona Beach racing moved to the new and demanding Daytona International Speedway in 1959, it was a stern test not only for the drivers, but also for the men building the race cars.

Hunter was there that first year and remembered the difficult task of putting a race car together to withstand the new track's high speeds and steep banking.

"We tried to talk to the driver about what worked best, but he didn't know, either, because everything was so new," Hunter said. "I found out one of the best ways to figure things out was to ride a motorcycle in the infield down near the corners and watch the cars slip through there. I'd change the chassis based on that."

$10 Gets You All This

Dorothy Beech was one of the originals. She never drove a lap in a race car, but she was involved in the foundation-building as NASCAR struggled through its early years.

Beech worked as a secretary who performed myriad tasks in the NASCAR office. She joined the organization in March 1951, only two years after founder Bill France Sr. ran the first season of what became Sprint Cup racing. At that point, the NASCAR office was in a two-room suite on a floor above a bank at 800 Main Street in Daytona Beach, Florida. The organization's first office had been in France's home in Daytona Beach at 29 Goodall Avenue.

"We were pretty small," Beech remembered. "There were only two of us working in the office when I started. We started the first newsletter when I was there. We used to cheer when the mail came in and we had a handful of [NASCAR] memberships."

It was relatively easy to be a NASCAR member in those days. For $10, you got a year's membership, a membership card, a car decal, a pin, regular newsletters, and coupons good for dollars off admission prices.

Beech remembered France Sr. as "such a big man, but he was so warm and friendly. He wasn't in town much because he was on the road at races and promoting races. I had no idea what a great promoter he was. When he got back to the office, he'd say hi to everybody. If he had picked up a good joke, he'd gather everybody around to tell it."

Go South, Young Man

More than a few racing people have been attracted to Florida by its weather. Sam Packard was one.

Packard arrived in Daytona Beach in 1945, not long after the end of World War II. He had been involved in racing in New England since 1937, and, after serving in the 82nd Airborne during the war, was looking for a new start.

"I had raced midgets in New England, but I heard about stock cars and that they were running on the beach [at Daytona Beach]," Packard said. "I decided to come down and get out of the snow and try out stock cars. I drove my pleasure car down [from Providence, Rhode Island] and got in the races. Being young and broke, I went to work for Bill France at his gas station."

France, who ran a service station at 316 Main Street in Daytona Beach, was working at the time to put some organizational structure in stock-car racing. In December 1947 he called numerous drivers and promoters to a series of meetings in Daytona Beach to talk about a new racing organization. Packard was among those in attendance as the group met for several hours each day in the lounge at the Streamline Hotel.

"We had been racing around the Carolinas and everything, and the promoters had been taking off with the money and leaving us stranded and so forth," Packard said. "With this organization, the promoter had to put money in escrow before we ever ran, so you were sure to get paid."

Once NASCAR was formed, Packard was named the NASCAR representative for New England. "Nobody knew what the hell it was all about," he said. "Eventually, we got to run NASCAR events up there."

It was a good deal for Packard, a man who had seen how it worked in the early days.

"I drove my personal car down to Daytona Beach three times from Providence to race it and once had to hitchhike home because I blew the engine," he said. "Now they have transporters to carry the cars that cost three times what my house does."

Wood Chopped Wood, Blazed Trails

Glen Wood, founder of one of the grandest teams in stock-car racing history, the Wood Brothers, got into motorsports innocently enough.

"I drove for the first time in 1950," Wood said. "A group of boys in town [Stuart, Virginia, where he lives to this day] decided to buy a little car and have fun with it. All of them backed out but me and Chris Williams [Wood's partner in a lumber business]. We bought a '38 Ford coupe and fixed it up. It had been wrecked. We paid $50 for it. We turned it into a race car."

Because Wood was in the lumber business, his racing nickname quickly became "the Woodchopper."

"We had a sawmill and sawed lumber for years," he said. "I went racing pretty much full-time while I was still in the lumber business. Racing was fun at first, but it gradually got to be a business. Before that, it was just a fun thing to do. You didn't plan to make a living out of it. It was nothing other than racing for fun. Most everybody who was in it had other ways to make dollars."

Wood blazed a trail of success along short tracks in the 1950s and early 1960s before retiring from driving as NASCAR moved into the superspeedway era.

"I didn't like the speeds that much," Wood said. "I just never particularly cared to go that fast. If I wasn't comfortable doing it, I'd rather let somebody that wanted to do it."

And there were a lot of famous "somebodies." The Wood Brothers team has a long history of hiring some of the best drivers in racing. The list includes Curtis Turner, Joe Weatherly, Junior Johnson, Ralph Earnhardt, Ned Jarrett, Fireball Roberts, Fred Lorenzen, Cale Yarborough, A.J. Foyt, David Pearson, and Dale Jarrett.

Let's Go Racing—in 1939

There was stock-car racing in various parts of the country years before NASCAR was formed in 1948.

Promoter Joe Littlejohn ran an automobile race at the Piedmont Interstate Fairgrounds' horse-racing track in his hometown of Spartanburg, South Carolina, on November 11, 1939. The half-mile track later would host NASCAR events, but making that first race in '39 a reality was a tough chore for Littlejohn, who went on to a career as a driver and track manager.

"I had gone to Daytona in 1938 and came back and thought there ought to be a track in Spartanburg," Littlejohn remembered. "I got to checking around and went to talk to city council about racing on the harness-racing track at the fair. They said, 'What in the world do you want to do, kill everybody in Spartanburg?' I said, 'No, I'm not planning on hurting anybody.'"

After finally getting the council's approval, Littlejohn scraped the track, packed it down, and covered it with calcium chloride in an attempt to control dust.

The race was run without incident, and thousands paid 75 cents to watch.

She Was a Doll, Baby

When Johnny Mantz drove to victory in the very first Southern 500 at Darlington Raceway in 1950, he rode the entire distance with a passenger.

Before the start of the grueling race, NASCAR's first on a big asphalt track, Mantz was given a small baby doll by a daughter of Alvin Hawkins, one of his team's owners.

Although Mantz qualified last in the massive 75-car field, he was able to conserve tires during the race and won easily, outrunning second-place Fireball Roberts by nine laps. Mantz survived the marathon, as did the doll.

The winning car—a 1950 Plymouth—and the good-luck doll can be seen in the museum at Darlington Raceway.

chapter 11

On the Air, Usually

Jack Smith stands by his 1958 Pontiac, which clearly advertises Atlanta Tune-Up Service. When TV cameras began covering races in the early 1950s, sponsorship and advertising on cars quickly followed.

In racing's early days, news-media coverage generally consisted of a handful of newspaper reporters sitting in a rickety wooden press box trying to report on a dust-covered racetrack with aging typewriters.

My, how things have changed. Television came on board in a big way in the 1970s and lifted NASCAR to new levels of interest, attracting fans who had never seen the sport in person.

Now NASCAR is so married to television that the start times of races are determined largely by network executives, and a huge traveling city of equipment and technicians follows the tour to every stop.

It has been a revolution.

A Disagreement in Turn 3

Much of the credit for NASCAR racing's stunning growth in the 1990s can be placed at the feet of television, which gave stock-car racing a new audience in places the sport had barely touched. ESPN, seeking programming to fill its schedule, and NASCAR, looking for a national broadcast partner, paired in 1981 to help each other, and among the results was a dramatic expansion of the NASCAR fan base.

A landmark moment in NASCAR history occurred in February 1979 as CBS offered flag-to-flag coverage of the Daytona 500, the sport's marquee race. In Turn 3 of the final lap, victory contenders Cale Yarborough and Donnie Allison crashed, giving the win to Richard Petty. As Petty celebrated, not quite ready to believe that he had actually won, Yarborough and Bobby Allison, who had stopped at the wreck site to check on his brother, engaged in fisticuffs, much to the entertainment of the television audience.

The incident obviously was controversial at the time, and the participants were hit with fines, but the publicity gave NASCAR a major national boost, and that race now is considered a turning point in the sport's move from a largely regional curiosity to national prominence.

Long before ESPN's arrival and the CBS Daytona gold strike, however, ABC gave NASCAR its first major television exposure. The network presented the first flag-to-flag coverage of a NASCAR Cup race on April 10, 1971, at Greenville-Pickens Speedway (GPS) in South Carolina. And it was a challenge.

ABC wanted to fit a full race into a 90-minute segment of its popular Saturday-afternoon *Wide World of Sports* program and started discussions about the prospects with NASCAR and GPS track owners Pete and Tom Blackwell, who operated one of the most successful short tracks in the sport.

"They were looking for a race they could get in, in an hour and a half," Pete Blackwell said. "They had gone through the result sheets from the year before and saw that we had finished a race in about an hour and 25 minutes. They asked me if I thought we could do that again. I said, 'Sure,' although there was no way I could be sure."

After the deal was made, NASCAR cut the starting field for the race from 30 cars to 26 in an effort to limit caution periods. It worked. The race was completed in one hour and 16 minutes, with Bobby Isaac taking the checkered flag first. The network found itself with extra time to fill.

Among the announcers on hand for the historic race were two men who would build sparkling careers in sports broadcasting—Jim McKay and Chris Economaki. Less visible—but just as important—that day was the technician in charge of making sure the signal feed reached New York City. Because of limited locations on the site, he was stationed in the restroom.

Change Two Tires and a Film Canister

Thanks to innovative camera technology that seems to be constantly evolving, television broadcasts of NASCAR races give viewers looks at action on the track from numerous angles.

In-car cameras show not only the racing from the driver's perspective but also how the driver reacts inside the car and, in some cases, his footwork as he moves through gear changes. Dozens of cameras are placed at key locations around and over (and sometimes in—as in buried in the asphalt) the track to show the competition from different viewpoints.

The technology is constantly racing forward and becoming smaller and smaller.

It was not always this way, as retired driver Larry Frank of Greenville, South Carolina, remembers.

During the 1964 and '65 Cup seasons, Frank, then a NASCAR regular, served as a camera operator for Paramount Pictures, which was producing *Red Line 7000*, a movie about NASCAR racing. The studio paid Frank to have a pair of movie cameras mounted on the front and rear of his 1964 Ford and, with

NASCAR's approval, Frank drove in Cup races and during practice sessions and filmed on-track action for the movie.

Although he was considered a competitor in the race and was scored the same as the other drivers, Frank didn't have a chance of winning during his film outings. He pitted every five to 10 laps (depending on the size of the track) to get a fresh canister of film.

Frank said he was paid $12,000 for his services, a paycheck that gave his racing team a substantial boost. "The crew got to eat regular meals and sleep on real beds for a change," he said.

Even Sportscasters Can Cry

The final race of the 1992 Cup season was a landmark moment in NASCAR history for several reasons.

Alan Kulwicki, who had come into Cup racing as an underfunded independent and stubbornly made his dream work, won the Cup championship that day at Atlanta Motor Speedway. Against all odds, and after turning down opportunities to drive for other teams, he won the championship with his own operation, despite lacking the resources of the series' leading teams.

On other fronts, that Atlanta race marked an arrival and a departure. It was Richard Petty's final race, which ended a long odyssey that began in the sport's formative years and was ending as it accelerated into national prominence. Even as Petty's driving career ended, Jeff Gordon's was beginning. Gordon made his first Cup start that day in Atlanta for Hendrick Motorsports. No one knew it then, but it was perfect symmetry—one champion leaving as another arrived.

ESPN broadcaster Jerry Punch was in the middle of all this history and had his hands full trying to handle the drama that unfolded before him.

"At the end of the race, I walked out to interview Alan, who's just pulled off the American dream," Punch said. "He had come into the sport with a pickup truck and pocket change. Then Richard Petty comes out of the garage for the final time in his career. I had tears running down my face, and he had tears in his. I don't think I had ever seen the King cry."

Everyone made it through it, but Punch still calls that day one of his most emotional in many years of sports coverage.

There's a Cicada in Turn 3!

It seems so easy, listening to them on the radio. Broadcasters describing the action on the track and in the pits at NASCAR races pass along information with seemingly little stress or apprehension, even as cars roar around and under them at remarkable speeds.

It isn't as simple as it looks, however.

Take the case of Chuck Carland, who works turns for the Performance Racing Network (PRN). At Bristol Motor Speedway at the annual night-race in the heat of August, Carland describes the action even as he battles the bugs and beetles of summer.

"At Bristol, Chuck ends up swallowing bugs, because all the lights are on," said Alicia Lingerfeldt, PRN director of broadcasting. "He has a bandana across his face. He looks like a bandit. Whenever you hear Chuck's voice crackling in Turn 3, he just swallowed a cicada."

Mike Bagley, who doubles as a Motor Racing Network producer and turn announcer, said every race can present new challenges for the guys who describe the action from seats of varying quality outside the turns. One of the most interesting, in the view of Bagley and others, is the tunnel turn at Pocono Raceway.

"From that position, you're picking cars up from three-quarters of a mile away," Bagley said. "You better take the binoculars. Then the exciting part is when they narrow up to go through the tunnel turn. I'm looking right down on top of the turn. A few cars have gotten away from drivers there. You can feel it when they hit the wall. I've had my bell rung a few times."

Bagley described working Turn 4 at Daytona as "pretty spectacular. You're watching the cars come up into the banking, and all of a sudden they come past you in about a second and a half. The wind rush is second to none."

Weather can have a big impact on announcers trying to describe a race from a perch around the turns. Atlanta Motor Speedway, which has often been plagued by rain and cold on race weekends, is one example.

"It seems like Atlanta is miserable most of the time," Carland said. "I'm on the top of the roof of the condos in Turn 4, and I get not only the regular wind, but the wind from in front of the condos coming up against me. I'm leaning off the edge of the condos, trying to get the best view. It can be the worst of elements.

"Turn 2 there also can be fun. I was working on a billboard there one year and forgot there was a gap between the walkway and the billboard and leaned back and fell through the crevice and barely caught myself."

At the inaugural race at Texas Motor Speedway in 1997, on a weekend hammered by rain, Carland found himself on scaffolding in Turn 4. "It was so muddy over there that the scaffolding started sliding down the banking with me on it during the race," he said.

That first race in Texas produced a plethora of wild stories from practically everyone involved in the wet and wild goings-on.

"It's funny to look back on now, but it was unbelievable there that week," Lingerfeldt said. "We got down there on Wednesday, and the cable we use to communicate—to get the broadcast signal to the satellite—was nowhere in sight. We had no way of getting on the air. And our [broadcast] gear got there late because the guy bringing it had a battery problem in his RV. He broke down in Louisiana and had to rent a U-Haul. At the track, Doug [Rice, PRN president] started yelling at a man who was about 6'6" and was bald with a long goatee and had just gotten out of prison. The guy's name was Killer or something. I thought, 'Doug is going to die.' Then Doug pulls out a big bottle of Mylanta and chugs it like it's liquor. Then we went to the infield, and a tornado touched down. And there was a 17-car wreck on the first lap of the race."

Just another radio broadcast.

TV Meant Money Even in the Early Days

Sponsorship is the fuel that keeps NASCAR going. Top teams now demand as much as $20 million a year for primary sponsorship, a figure needed to keep organizations fully funded and in possession of the best equipment.

Those kinds of numbers stagger people who were involved in stock-car racing in its pioneer years. Many cars in the early days carried no sponsorship at all; others might have picked up a few dollars for painting "Joe's Car Wash" on the sides of their race vehicles.

Sponsors eventually became as competitive as the race teams, however, each trying to latch on to the best teams and gain the best exposure for their products or services.

Hall of Fame driver Jack Smith saw a very early example of sponsor competition in 1952, his fourth year in the sport.

"I was racing at the Peach Bowl in Atlanta, and Channel 5 came out and televised some of the races," Smith remembered. "The first night I won the race. I was advertising Bishop Brothers Used Cars in Atlanta. My car stood out under the lights. That was good for television. A manager of another used-car dealership came to me after the race and said if I put R.S. Evans Used Cars on my car, he'd give me $500 a night. My eyes got real big.

"I talked to the Bishops, and they said, 'Well, if they can do it, we can, too.' So I started getting $500. Evans came back and offered $1,000 a night three races later.

"I said right then that if racing ever really got on television, there'd be no limit to where it would go."

Earnhardt at Tailback?

Eli Gold has his feet—or, to be more accurate, his mouth—in two worlds. And each has its own collection of rabid fans.

Gold is the play-by-play broadcaster for the University of Alabama football team. He also works frequently on NASCAR radio broadcasts and has a longtime connection to stock-car racing.

His travel schedule is often hectic, for obvious reasons. He also broadcasts National Football League and Arena Football League games, does weekly fan call-in shows, and has broadcast professional hockey, college basketball, and minor league baseball.

Sometimes, Gold has to remind himself where he is.

"People have asked if I've ever said the quarterback handed off to Earnhardt," Gold said. "One year at Dover, I almost did the wrong network ID. I almost said, 'This is the Crimson Tide Sports Network instead of Motor Racing Network.' I hadn't had much sleep."

Gold did his first NASCAR broadcast in 1976, and he became Alabama's football play-by-play man in 1988.

And he's from, of all places, Brooklyn, New York.

"To say I would ever imagine a kid from Brooklyn doing all this, you couldn't even allow yourself to think like that," Gold said.

ESPN, NASCAR Strong Partners

ESPN, which became a partner with NASCAR in 1981 and dramatically increased nationwide exposure of stock-car racing, broadcast races for 20 years before giving way to other networks. ESPN returned to the NASCAR fold in 2007.

ESPN's first run with NASCAR lifted both racing's visibility and its bottom line. The network was on board for some of racing's biggest moments—Harry Gant's four straight wins late in the 1991 season, Dale Jarrett's first win at Michigan in 1991, and the final race of the 1992 season, which was Richard Petty's final event and Jeff Gordon's first.

Martinsville Speedway president Clay Campbell said the first ESPN contract with his track resulted in a $20,000 check for Martinsville. "And I thought I had died and gone to heaven," Campbell said.

"ESPN came in and took this to another level. Prior to that, you had segments on ABC's *Wide World of Sports* and maybe a few races on CBS. You couldn't ask for a better partner than what ESPN was for us at that time. They legitimized our sport and brought it to a lot of people who otherwise wouldn't know what NASCAR was. It opened the door for a lot of things to happen, and then when Fox and NBC came in, they kicked the door down.

"ESPN pretty much revolutionized the in-car cameras. The talent they had was phenomenal. They knew the sport, and everything they did was top-notch."

Delaying the Olympics

What's the best race finish in NASCAR history?

That's a topic that can lead to hours of spirited debate, but one that certainly must rank in the top five of all-time is the finish of the 1976 Daytona 500, a race that saw the two giants of the sport at the time—Richard Petty and David Pearson—take their rivalry to its highest point. And an unusual part of the story that day is that television, then in its infancy in covering NASCAR, had to react swiftly to respond to the drama.

Although all NASCAR Cup races are broadcast from start to finish these days, in the 1970s coverage was spotty at best. For the 1976 Daytona 500, ABC had reached an agreement with NASCAR to televise the concluding portion of the race live.

As the race reached its climax, the fight for the win turned into a Pearson-Petty duel, as it had so many times in that decade.

Even as Petty took the lead with 13 laps to go, ABC technical personnel prepared to shift their focus at the end of the race from Daytona Beach, Florida, to Innsbruck, Austria, where the network was broadcasting the Winter Olympics. Within minutes after the race, coverage of the Olympics was scheduled to begin.

Dennis Lewin, a coordinating producer for ABC, was on the line with Roone Arledge, a producer at the ABC Olympics site in Innsbruck.

"He asked me if we were going to run over into the Olympics' time," Lewin said. "I told him, no, that everything was fine.

Everything was going along as expected. Then—wham!—so much for that."

In the 500's final lap, Pearson drove within inches of Petty's first-place Dodge, looking for an opening. He found it entering Turn 3 and passed Petty. Petty reacted immediately, dropped low between Turns 3 and 4, and pulled alongside Pearson as they charged through the last turn with the checkered flag in sight.

As they left the turn and ran onto the track's tri-oval, their cars touched and slammed into the outside wall. Pearson's car bounced to the inside, and Petty's spun out of control and finally came to a stop on the grass that separated the race course from pit road.

Before the grandstand crowd could fully absorb what had happened, Pearson, who had had the foresight to push in his clutch during the accident to keep the engine running, drove his car onto the asphalt at about 20 mph and chugged past Petty to take the checkered flag first, scoring one of the slowest major victories in NASCAR history.

ABC had a great show, and the Olympics had to wait.

"We stayed with the race and ran over several minutes into the Olympics' time," Lewin said.

chapter 12

Toil, Trouble, and No Kissing, Please

Carl Edwards turns his signature postwin backflip after winning the NASCAR Nationwide Series Missouri-Illinois Dodge Dealers 250 on July 19, 2008, at Gateway International Raceway in Madison, Illinois.

When you've been racing for six decades on virtually every kind of racetrack, some bizarre stuff is bound to happen.

Off the track, too, there have been some unusual tales.

And the Winner Is...We Dunno

One of the biggest scoring mistakes in NASCAR history—as admitted by then–NASCAR president Bill France Jr.—occurred at Atlanta Motor Speedway in the 1978 Dixie 500.

NASCAR officials named Alabama driver Donnie Allison the race winner at 7:40 PM, three hours and 10 minutes after the race's conclusion. In the interim period, NASCAR had declared Richard Petty the winner after waving the checkered flag over Allison. A second check of the scoring cards—this was before computerized scoring—revealed an omitted lap on Allison's card, and the victory was returned to him.

Oddly enough, Brian France, now NASCAR's chairman but then a 16-year-old odd-job worker for his father's organization, was involved on the fringes of the decision.

Brian France approached Hoss Ellington, the owner of Allison's car, in the garage area after Petty had celebrated the win with his teammates. "You won the race," Brian France told Ellington. "A lady scoring your car screwed up. She was yelling for Petty all day. I was scoring Bobby Allison's car, and there was another girl sitting next to me scoring your car. They [NASCAR officials] grabbed her card during the race and kept trying to make the two match. They never could.

"While they were grabbing and shuffling things around, they were missing stuff. They knew they were in trouble 15 laps from the end of the race."

Allison finished the race three car lengths in front of Petty and Dave Marcis, who apparently was second. Petty beat Marcis to the finish line by a few feet as the crowd of 40,000 roared. A win would have ended a 42-race winless streak for Petty.

But a NASCAR official informed the Petty crew as the checkered flag dropped that Allison had won, and Petty crew chief Dale Inman told Petty by two-way radio to go to the garage area instead of victory lane. Allison drove his Chevrolet to victory lane, but confusion reigned, and a frenzied check of the scorecards began.

NASCAR officials announced at 6:30 PM, two hours after the race, that the card-check showed Allison one lap down, thus giving Petty the victory. Petty and his team members celebrated the win in a makeshift victory lane in the track's garage area.

Later, Ellington and Petty joined NASCAR officials to check the scorecards again.

Allison, who had said he was certain that he had won, left the track after Petty's win was announced.

Bill France Jr. described the situation as "an all-time NASCAR screw-up on scoring. We decided Richard was the winner in going over and over the scorecards. But we kept going over them and came up with the correct answer. I want to apologize to Donnie Allison, Richard Petty, and to the fans."

The race also featured another odd occurrence. Twenty-seven of the event's first 35 laps were run under caution while speedway fire units were moved outside the track to aid in the battle against a grass fire in one of the speedway's parking areas. The fire destroyed about 20 cars before several area fire departments and speedway personnel extinguished it.

You Can't Outrace a Bug

It was to be one of the biggest social events of the 2006 NASCAR season—the July 29 wedding of driver Kurt Busch and his fiancée, Eva Bryan.

Very visible as a couple at race sites for many months, Busch and Bryan scheduled their wedding ceremony on a beach at Chesapeake Bay, Virginia. They planned to have a pier and dock built at the site for the wedding and reception, but tiger beetles intervened.

The beetles' mating season occurs in that area in June and July, and some environmentalists said that constructing the pier and dock near the water could have a negative impact on the beetles' activities.

Rather than fight a battle of that sort on their wedding weekend, Busch and Bryan moved the ceremony to a friend's home in Virginia Beach, Virginia.

Edwards Backflips into the Future

Carl Edwards' backflip has become an expected part of the post-race ritual when he wins. It's not unique in sports, but in auto racing you just don't see that many drivers leaping off race cars into the air and turning a flip in the sky.

Edwards learned the particulars of the flip from a former girlfriend who was a gymnast, but his inspiration came from two other sources—one a racer and the other a baseball player.

"The first guy I saw do something like that was Ozzie Smith [retired St. Louis Cardinals shortstop who often showcased his acrobatic skills on the field]," Edwards said. "I thought that was the neatest thing in the world. You always think of a backflip as something that a gymnast does, and I see a guy out there on a baseball field doing it. Tyler Walker is the first race-car driver I saw do it, and I thought it was so neat that I worked on it a little bit.

"We went to Capital Speedway in Holts Summit [Missouri] one night, and we won the race. I jumped up on the back of the race car and did one, and the kids loved it. It's just a way to show how excited I am to win. As long as they like it, I'll do it."

Busch Brothers Become Bash Brothers

There have been family connections in NASCAR since its beginning.

There have been the Pettys—Lee, Richard, Kyle, and Adam; the Allisons—Bobby, Donnie, and Davey; the Pearsons—David, Larry, Ricky, and Eddie; the Labontes—Terry and Bobby; the Bakers—Buck and Buddy; and on and on. The roster is almost limitless.

It's simple arithmetic that, with fathers, sons, and brothers competing on the same track, family ties are going to be tested now and then. In the 2007 Nextel All-Star Challenge at Lowe's Motor Speedway, brothers Kurt and Kyle Busch crashed dramatically while racing for position and needed a conversation afterward to smooth things over.

Brothers Ward and Jeff Burton also have raced for position in Cup competition, but Jeff said they got their brother-versus-brother incidents out of the way before they reached the big time.

"Ward and I went through that at a local level, when we were on different pages with where we were in our lives at that point," Jeff said. "We didn't understand that racing isn't more important than family. And we learned the hard way. But we did it in front of maybe 1,000 people [at a Virginia short track], not millions of people.

"That's one of the great advantages of being able to grow up and being in this major scene is that you can make mistakes without it being so glaring. Ward and I had a time when we didn't understand how to race against each other and still have a lot of respect for each other. There'll be a day when it becomes clear to any brothers that family is more important. And, hopefully, it doesn't have to get ugly before you realize that."

The All-Star Race wasn't the first time the Busch brothers had tangled. There also was what Kurt Busch called "the Castle Rock Court 500," so named after the street where they grew up. Kurt was 14 and Kyle was seven, and their father, Tom, let them race in go-carts.

"My dad said five laps," Kurt said. "That last lap was out, so I got back in front of Kyle going into Turn 1. Down the back straightaway I'm leading, so I started counting my chickens. I've got this thing in the bag. Coming off Turn 4, I feel this nudge to the left rear. He climbs over the left-rear tire and knocks the carburetor off my go-cart. Now I don't have any power to get back to the start/finish line, and he wins the race.

"It was like in my mind I had won the race because he had just clobbered me and wrecked me and took the power out of my car.

He looked back at me and said, 'You know what, I got back to the start/finish line first, so I won.'"

Hey, I Can Do That

A son and grandson of race-car drivers, Kyle Petty has an inquisitive interest in the history of stock-car racing, in particular the way drivers choose to enter the sport.

Petty said he understands the attraction for sons and brothers of racers. "The family always has been involved, so it's just a natural thing," he said. But what about drivers with no family background in the sport?

Petty, who also has worked as a commentator on television racing broadcasts, interviewed David Pearson, the second-winningest Cup driver of all time and a key rival of Petty's father, Richard, about that topic.

"He said, 'My daddy took me to Daytona [in the 1950s], and we were standing on the beach watching a race [on the old Daytona beach-road course],'" Petty said. "He said, 'We saw Cotton Owens come by, and he had some kind of little helmet and goggles on and his arm hanging out of the car, real casual like. Damn, if he didn't win the race. I said, "Hell, I can do that."'"

And he did. Pearson won 105 races—some of them driving for Owens, oddly enough—and three Cup championships. He is recognized by many as the best stock-car racer of all time.

A Driver Learns to Talk Good

It's virtually a given now that every successful Sprint Cup driver is also a good public speaker—comfortable in front of a microphone, steady in the spotlight. Some have gone on to become stars on national-television broadcasts of races, and others—notably Jeff Gordon—have crossed over into the entertainment field.

It wasn't always that way, of course. Some drivers come to the top level of the sport still trying to make themselves at home as a center of attention. Some of their speaking skills need a few more practice laps.

Geoffrey Bodine knows the drill. As his NASCAR driving career began to build, he worked at refining the rough parts of his résumé.

"In 1976 I had to speak at a roast for a guy in Hartford, Connecticut," he said. "I'll never forget that night. It was the most humiliating thing I'd ever been through, but I realized that I needed some help with my public speaking. I signed up for a Dale Carnegie course. But I never went. I never had the time.

"So I went out and bought some books on public speaking. I still have them on the shelf, all those books. And I watched Richard Petty and Darrell Waltrip and picked out the good things they did and the not-so-good things I did, and together with my reading I self-taught myself. I came out of my shell. That night in Hartford could have put me deeper in my shell, but I turned it around and made it a positive, and I'm kind of proud of that."

Everybody Meet in Clint's Backyard

Not everybody has the opportunity to race in the backyard.

Clint Bowyer does. As he began to find success in NASCAR racing after hooking up with car owner Richard Childress, Bowyer brought part of the excitement home. He built a one-eighth-mile go-cart dirt track behind his house in Clemmons, North Carolina.

Bowyer, his Richard Childress Racing teammates, other RCR employees, and assorted friends and hangers-on compete at Muddy Creek International Speedway, so named because of the stream that runs near Bowyer's house.

"Racing has always been a 'family' sport for me," Bowyer said. "I believe in keeping all the guys together and pulling as one as a team. It's another way to get everybody together during the week and keep a smile on their faces. These guys were racing the carts in the parking lot at RCR before I even got there, so this was a natural thing to do."

Bowyer lives close to his boss, Richard Childress, who, as Bowyer puts it, owns "some formidable farm equipment." Bowyer borrowed that equipment to cut the track from the woods behind his house using a tape measure, common sense, and a big dirt-mover.

It's the dream of many race fans to build their own tracks. It isn't as easy as moving dirt around, though. Bowyer cleared trees and underbrush to create open space, flattened and fine-tuned the track area, then built the turns. Before each race evening, he grooms the track.

"It's a great place to blow off some steam," Bowyer said. "All the guys come ready to race. If one of them does something special to his cart and does well that week, you can bet that everybody else will be trying it the next week."

The Day Petty Went Industrial-Size

Through NASCAR's six decades, the sport's competitors have challenged the rule book in almost every way imaginable.

Some call it cheating. Others say it's simply "gettin' competitive." It has gone on, literally, from the first race in 1949 to the present day, and, despite the growth of NASCAR's inspector ranks and the increasing sophistication of its inspection process, some impressive rule-bending will still get through.

What's the biggest rule-challenging circumstance in NASCAR history? That might be a matter of debate, but most historians would pick the Petty Enterprises team's use of a larger-than-allowed engine in Richard Petty's 1983 victory in the fall race at what was then Charlotte Motor Speedway.

After Petty's car won the race, inspectors measured his engine at 392 cubic inches, considerably bigger than the 358 allowed. Additionally, the team had put left-side tires on the car's right side, another significant violation.

The scandal rocked the sport, in large part because Petty already had won seven championships and had long been considered one of racing's good guys. He was penalized 104 series points and fined $35,000, at that time the largest monetary penalty in NASCAR history, but he kept the victory.

Maurice Petty, Richard's brother and the team's engine builder, took the blame for the incident but hinted that other teams also were toying with the rule book.

For many years to come, that game continued, and many other infractions were caught, which resulted in even bigger penalties. But Petty's run with the big engine will continue to stand out in NASCAR "police" history.

Mast: "Wide Open and Sliding"

Like many other NASCAR racers, retired driver Rick Mast started driving before the law said he could.

As Mast remembers it, he was 12 years old. "My mom and dad would go to the movies, and I was by myself," he said. "We had an old Mercury Comet. It had a three-speed on the column. I'd hop in that thing and tear off down the road. I could go all the way to Stanton [Virginia, about 35 miles from his home] on dirt roads with the exception of about three miles. I don't know how in the world I ever survived. It was always wide open and sliding. I never did get caught. How, I don't have a clue."

When Mast got on the road legally, he went through a series of the cool cars of the period. "I had a 1957 Chevrolet, a 1964 Chevelle four-door, and a 1969 Road Runner," he said. "The '64 Chevelle—it would run down the road a ways, maybe 10 miles, and stop and quit. Just quit. I never could figure out why."

It Will Be a Cold Day When I Race There

Jerry Nadeau is perhaps the only NASCAR driver who has raced on ice in Russia.

Yes, ice.

A former star in go-cart racing, Nadeau was invited to run against some of the best of the rest of the world on an ice track.

"My first lap on the track, I put one of the carts right over the snowbank up on my roof," Nadeau said. "That was before I learned how to do it without using any brakes. You just kind of get on the gas and bounce off the snowbanks. I won two races out of eight, had two seconds, and the rest were all wrecks.

"We went over there and raced against Russians, Swedes, Finns, people from several countries. It was quite an experience. Most of them had done it before. It was my first time there, and it was a lot of fun, but I got food poisoning and was sick 10 days straight. It was tough, but, all in all, it was one of the weirdest and greatest experiences I've ever had."

He Ain't Heavy, He's Bobby's Brother

When Bobby Labonte won the NASCAR Cup championship in 2000, he reached a remarkable milestone.

Although family connections—the Pettys, the Allisons, the Pearsons, the Waltrips, the Flocks—have been standard throughout NASCAR history, Labonte's title made him one-half of the first brother combination to win championships. Terry, Bobby's older brother, was the Cup champion in 1984 and 1996.

"That's a great feeling," Labonte said. "To be racing with Terry now, to be competitive with him, to go from watching him race hobby stocks at Corpus Christi [Texas] Speedway when he was 15 and I was eight, watching them tear down a '57 Chevy.

"I can remember those days, so I guess that's what makes it all special. We've raced for a long time now. To be a part of winning the championship—both of us, I think that's just overwhelming for our family."

It Wouldn't Handle a Lick

In a long, eventful, and successful NASCAR career, Bobby Allison was involved in a long list of accidents—some of his making, most made by others. One of those, at Pocono Raceway in 1988, ultimately ended his driving career and almost cost him his life.

Prior to that crash, one of Allison's worst wrecks occurred at North Carolina Speedway in Rockingham, North Carolina, in 1976.

Pinched by other cars on the track's backstretch, Allison's car launched into the air, bounced off another car, and then began a wicked sequence of rolls.

Allison jumped out of the car with minor injuries, although he visited the track's infield care center to have glass removed from his eyes.

He kept his sense of humor, though. "I knew I was in trouble when I got upside down," he said. "The car quit handling."

Watch Out for Those Shoes

David Pearson raced in NASCAR from 1960 to 1986 and, remarkably, was never seriously injured.

"I've never been taken to the hospital, never even rode in an ambulance," Pearson said.

Some of that was luck, of course, but Pearson, a 105-race winner, also had an uncanny ability to be in the right place at the right time. He was a master at avoiding wrecks and of seeing them forming early enough to put himself in position to be safe.

"I've heard people say that if you see a car spin out, you should head toward it and it'll be gone by the time you get there," Pearson said. "That's a bunch of bull. I never did head for it. When there's a wreck, you see a bunch of people spin out a long time before they get there. That's crazy. I'd just start slowing down and get as slow as I could until I got to where the wreck was and then make a decision whether I was going right or left. You keep your car as straight as you can keep it."

David Pearson, who had an almost preternatural knack for being at the right place at the right time, poses with some admirers after winning the Rebel 500 at Darlington on April 11, 1976.

Pearson's worst wreck? It happened at Bristol, Tennessee, he said.

"I was driving for Holman-Moody, and my wheels got locked up with Marvin Panch's car," he said. "Neither one of us could get turned coming off 4, and I hit the wall hard. It tore the car up, and it knocked my shoes off, I hit so hard—the hardest I ever hit, I guess.

"It scared me because my shoes were off. I'd always heard when people were killed in a car wreck that it knocked their shoes off. They were laying there just like I had placed them there, side by side. I couldn't wait until somebody came and talked to me so I could answer them and see if they'd talk back. I didn't know if I was dead or not."

What's in a Number?

Richard Petty will forever be identified with the No. 43 because he drove cars with that number through most of his racing career. Jeff Gordon has the same attachment to No. 24 and the late Dale Earnhardt to the famous, forward-facing No. 3.

Although drivers are more likely to change numbers in modern times due to switching sponsors and/or teams, most would prefer to stay with a particular number, often because of a strong childhood connection.

"Car numbers mean a great deal to a driver," said Jeff Burton, who raced No. 99 at Roush Racing and No. 31 for Richard Childress Racing. "I look back with great fondness when I ran Late Model and when I first ran the Busch Series. I ran No. 12 because that was my dad's number. That's the number he wore when he was in high school. That was the number that my brothers raced with.

"I was No. 11 when I was racing go-karts, and that was Cale Yarborough's number. Numbers are a reflection of something for everybody. Everybody looks at a number differently, but, without question, a number is a really important thing. That's how people relate to you."

Burton Escapes to the Cove

Ward Burton has been saving the world—or at least a big chunk of it—for more than a decade.

The piece he's most concerned about is a 1,123-acre tract near Clover, Virginia, in his old stomping grounds. The spread, called "the Cove," is the golden center of the Ward Burton Wildlife Foundation, a nonprofit organization Burton founded in 1996 with the idea of saving rural and forest lands from encroaching development.

Burton, who has been at home in the outdoors since his childhood, manages the Cove, develops usage plans for the property, and seeks to expand it by buying adjacent land. Burton's efforts have attracted the attention of the Natural Resources Conservation Service (a division of the United States Department of Agriculture), which sent some of its top officials to the Cove to assist in the dedication of a wetland-restoration project.

The property is sacred ground for Burton. As a 10-year-old, he and his father and grandfather walked the woods in the area. The property was then owned by C.R. Sanders, a friend of the Burton family.

Sanders and C.H. Watts, another property-owner in the area, became close friends with Burton and asked him to oversee the property and to protect it after their deaths.

"This land kind of fell into my hands to take care of as I got older, and I really started seeing the importance of this place beyond the fact that I love it so much," said Burton, who lived in the Cove woods for several years while he tried to determine a path for his life. "It's like sacred ground to me. I didn't have a plan when I was a youngster walking these woods. Now it's turned into my life mission."

When Burton began seriously working on the property in the 1980s, he knew little about proper approaches to conservation. "I bought my first tractor and started working the land," he said. "I started learning. I wasn't brought up around a tractor. I just started doing it. I learned to disc and lime and how to take a soil sample. I learned by doing. I've learned the whole time, and I'm still learning. I'll go to my deathbed still not knowing it all. It's about forestry management, clean air, clear water. You're always a learner. There's always something else."

Burton sees himself as a conservationist.

"Preservation—and there are places for that—is when you have land and you let Mother Nature take care of its state," he said. "You don't ride a four-wheeler on it. You don't drive a truck on it. In some places, that's good. On the other side, conservation is working with the forest instead of letting the forest do its thing. If we want to sustain our oak forests, we know through science how to sustain them. One way is to take out some of the smaller trees so the ground gets sunlight and starts to grow small oaks. Through expertise and education and the willingness to do a little work, we can make the habitat better than what Mother Nature has."

Burton's ideas are working. Rabbits, deer, turkeys, bobcats, raccoons, skunks, a wide assortment of birds, and other creatures roam the property, along with black bears, who have wandered north from the North Carolina coastal plain. Bald eagles frequent the Cove's tall trees.

Burton foresees multiple uses for the property as it continues to age and grow, but he sees his primary role as that of steward and educator, particularly for the students and children's groups that visit the Cove. The plans include the building of a welcome/education center. Working with government grants, grants from other foundations, and donations from sponsor companies and individuals, Burton hopes to enhance and expand the Cove over the next 10 years.

He also plans to keep his hands in racing.

Ambrose a Long Way from Home

Australian Marcos Ambrose put his car on the road toward Formula One but wound up parking in the NASCAR garage. And he's quite happy, thank you.

Ambrose won multiple carting championships in Australia and, with the support of his family, moved into Formula Ford competition in 1996 with the idea of ultimately advancing to Formula One. He finished second in Formula Ford racing in 1997 and jumped to Europe in 1998 to pursue his dream in earnest.

He had some success in Formula racing in France and England but couldn't position himself to get a good shot at Formula One. He returned to Australia in 2000 and quickly reestablished himself on the racing scene there.

"I had committed my money and my family's money [in the F1 effort]," Ambrose said. "I lost some chasing a dream. I either ran out of talent, time, or money in Europe. I couldn't work out which came first. But I learned a lot there. I stuck to it as long as I could to try and make the best of the situation. We won a lot of races and drove some great cars."

Back at home, Ambrose won the Supercar championship in 2003 and 2004 and, along the way, built a strong relationship with Ford Motor Co. That connection gave him his shot at NASCAR.

"I was making good money as a two-time Supercar champion," Ambrose said. "I turned my back on it and walked away. I was with the best team and had a pretty healthy Ford contract, a huge fan base, and strong sponsor support. I was willing to sacrifice that. I walked away because I wanted to. I didn't want to grow old and regret not having a go.

"I had itchy feet [in Australia]. I looked up to NASCAR and was a big fan of it. Anybody who is serious about racing will tell you that NASCAR is the biggest thing in racing. It was just a natural progression to try it. There was a lot of good timing and good luck involved. I took advantage of my situation as a Ford driver in Australia. I won a couple of championships with them and got to know Dan Davis [then Ford's motorsports director] well."

In 2005 Ambrose was introduced to Busch Series team owner Tad Geschickter during a race in Indianapolis, and Ambrose stayed in contact with him. Two months later, Ambrose ran tests with the team, and the results were positive. Ambrose moved his family to Charlotte, North Carolina, and joined Geschickter's Craftsman Truck Series team.

It's Ambrose's second international journey in search of racing stardom. "We came from a world away for this," he said. "I keep telling my friends there, they have to come and check this out. It's a surreal thing for me to be here from my origins."

No Autograph for You

NASCAR drivers are hounded perpetually by autograph seekers, but Matt Kenseth can be forgiven for being more than a little upset at a fan who sought his signature in 2007 at Watkins Glen International in New York.

The race was red-flagged for cleanup of an accident, and the field was sitting on the track. Suddenly, a fan ran from the stands across the grass separating the seating area from the track, jumped a barrier, and went directly to the passenger side of Kenseth's car. He then asked Kenseth to sign his cap.

Kenseth, somewhat startled by the incident, refused to sign, saying he was somewhat busy.

The fan was apprehended and arrested.

Matt Kenseth is usually more than happy to sign autographs for fans before and after races, but that was not the case when one bungling fan sought out his signature during a race.

Redskins Join Cowboys?

It was perhaps the ultimate example of cats sleeping with dogs.

Former Dallas Cowboys quarterbacks Roger Staubach and Troy Aikman teamed in 2006 to join the NASCAR circuit, starting a team called Hall of Fame Racing. Because they were new to the sport and had no technical base from which to build a team, they signed a working agreement with established team owner Joe Gibbs to give them a head start.

Gibbs, of course, was the head coach of the Washington Redskins, the Cowboys' biggest rivals. To say the least, it was an unusual partnership.

"[People] say, 'Gosh, how do you team up with a Redskin?'" Aikman said. "Or, they're asking Joe Gibbs, 'How in the world do you team up with two Cowboys?' Whereas, I look at it like it makes great sense, because we both have the NFL connection, and we both have this great interest in NASCAR. So this is a perfect marriage between the two organizations.

"Obviously, when we played each other, there was a tremendous rivalry between us and the Redskins, and we had a lot of great battles with Joe Gibbs."

A Weird Day at the Rock

The October 1995 race was one of the strangest ever held at North Carolina Speedway, the Rockingham, North Carolina, track known as "the Rock."

Although the event resulted in Ward Burton scoring the first win of his Cup career, it was perhaps most remembered for a wacky series of screwups.

After Dale Earnhardt made a pit stop, he was black-flagged because a NASCAR inspector thought the team failed to put on a lug nut during a tire change. When Earnhardt rolled into his pit, all five lug nuts were tight. Thirty-seven laps later, after discussion,

NASCAR threw a caution flag to return Earnhardt to the track position he had held before the mistake.

During the caution period, pit road was closed, but Earnhardt and several other drivers pitted, which enhanced the confusion. NASCAR then lengthened the caution to allow other drivers to pit.

In an unusual move, NASCAR president Bill France Jr. visited the speedway press box after the race to explain the problem—and the corrective measures—to journalists.

A Language Barrier—in the House

It's one of the great mysteries of NASCAR racing, and it involves two brothers.

Ward and Jeff Burton were raised in South Boston, Virginia, by the same parents and in the same house. They're both good ol' Southern boys, but there's one big difference between them—Ward speaks with a distinctive, syrupy Virginia drawl, while Jeff's speech is more middle-of-the-road and decidedly not like his brother's.

What happened?

"Maybe I was brought up in the south end of the house, and he was in the northern side," said Ward, repeating reasoning that both he and Jeff have used over the years when questioned about the topic.

"I don't know why we speak differently," Jeff said. "The blood tests are definitive. We are brothers. No one really understands it. My parents don't understand it. I don't understand it."

Generally speaking, though, more people understand Jeff than Ward.

The Money's Nice, but...

It's abundantly clear that success in auto racing allows the sport's top drivers to own huge homes, fancy cars, and fast airplanes.

But are these guys in it for the money? Although the extravagant lifestyles certainly are nice, most say they'd race only for trophies. And some can become downright indignant when their motives are questioned.

"I think that people see the big houses, and they see the big airplanes, and they see nice motor homes, and they think that's why you're racing," said Jeff Burton, one of NASCAR's most articulate drivers. "The reason that we have the airplanes and houses and motor homes is because we can. I'm not aware of any of my friends that, when we have conversations about racing, the topic of money comes up.

"We are very well paid, as we should be. You can make a case that we're overpaid, and I'm okay if people think we're overpaid. But I've never sat in a race car thinking, 'This is how much money I'm going to make today.' Just because we make the money doesn't mean that's why we do it.

"I'm not here because I make every dime I can. I'm here because I love it. It's my passion. It's what I want to do. I have enough money. I don't have to do this. I could quit today if I wanted to.... I love to race, and when I talk to the Matt Kenseths and the Mark Martins and the Kevin Harvicks and the Clint Bowyers, money is something that we make because we can. I get a little perturbed about it, because just because we have those things doesn't mean that's why we're here."

A Dream Come True

Kurt Busch owns a photograph that shows him and his father, Tom, attending Kurt's first NASCAR Cup race on November 3, 1991, at Phoenix International Raceway.

Kurt was 13 and already racing on short tracks, but he was excited to be able to see the cars and stars of the Cup Series up close. Ironically, the photograph of the Busches shows them standing in the pit of driver Rusty Wallace, who drove the No. 2 Penske car. Years later, Busch would replace Wallace as the car's driver.

"There I am, way back then as a skinny little kid, standing in front of Rusty's pit area before the start of the race and posing in front of the Miller Genuine Draft pit box," Busch said. "That's pretty cool to think about that day way back then and see how far we've been able to come."

Only Taxis Can Speed in NYC

One of the highlights of NASCAR's annual end-of-the-season celebration in New York City has become the parade lap along Big Apple streets that the circuit's top drivers make to celebrate their season of success.

The fun was tempered a bit after the 2005 run through the streets, however. Ryan Newman took advantage of the occasion to smoke his tires and burn a donut during the parade, which irritated some higher-ups in the New York Police Department.

Before the top 10 drivers took to the streets the following season, they were told that no such shenanigans would take place.

"They didn't threaten us with anything, but they just asked us to remember that it's a special thing for NASCAR, and a lot of work has gone into it, and it would be really foolish if any of us acted like fools out there and messed it up," said seasonal champion Jimmie Johnson.

The parade included a little bumping—mostly courtesy of Matt Kenseth, but the drivers brought the cars home without serious incident.

The city was safe.

Money in the Ground?

What do drivers do with those whopping big checks they get for winning races?

Jimmie Johnson had more than a few ideas for handling a million-dollar check for winning the All-Star Race at Lowe's Motor Speedway. And one of them was an old-timer's approach.

"Maybe I'd go buy myself an old car," Johnson said. "I have been collecting old cars for a while now. I need a Harley, so I'd like to get a motorcycle. Maybe I would go spoil myself with something like that.

"Then I could dig a hole in the backyard and bury the rest and forget about it."

Fired Up at the Ballpark

One of the most unusual marriages in professional sports was celebrated in the summer of 2007 at one of Major League Baseball's most cherished facilities—Fenway Park in Boston.

Boston Red Sox team owner John Henry became a partner with Jack Roush in Roush's NASCAR operation, and the partnership was the focus of Roush Fenway Racing Night at Fenway Park on June 29, 2007.

The history of Fenway Park, Major League Baseball's oldest stadium, is filled with some of the most dramatic moments in baseball's long run as one of America's favorite sports. On this night, however, history of a different sort was made.

Mike Lanier drove a Roush Fenway Racing show-car decorated with Red Sox insignia from underneath the park's centerfield seats and onto the warning track. He stopped near home plate, delivered the first baseballs for that night's game, and then circled the field.

It was the first time a race car had entered the hallowed space of Fenway.

Also as part of the night's festivities, Roush and team driver Carl Edwards threw out the first pitch of the evening.

Sorry, No Kissing before Races

Superstition doesn't play much of a role in NASCAR racing in modern times, but there were times when drivers went out of their ways to avoid things they considered potentially detrimental to success.

Two of the biggest superstitions in racing involved peanuts in the pits and the color green. Both were considered very bad luck. You still don't see many peanuts along pit row these days, but the idea that green carried bad vibes began disappearing in the 1970s when green sponsors like Mountain Dew and Gatorade demanded that their cars carry their colors.

Fireball Roberts, the sport's first superstar driver, was also among its most superstitious. In the early 1950s Roberts had a bad crash in a race, and he later blamed that accident on the fact that a beauty queen had kissed him before the event started. Roberts told friends that he didn't allow any woman—even his wife—to kiss him prior to a race after that incident.

Roberts perhaps adjusted his attitude in February 1962 at the Daytona 500. Mary Ann Mobley, formerly a Miss America and bound for a career as an actress, was Miss Speed Weeks that year, and she kissed Roberts on the cheek before the race.

Roberts breezed to his first win in the 500 despite the Mobley hex.

That's Sterling, with a *G*

Before Sterling Marlin became a star driver in the NASCAR Cup Series, he was a track champion and consistent race winner at Nashville Raceway near his hometown.

It was at the speedway that there first developed a minicontroversy about Marlin's first name. Marlin liked *Sterlin* (without the *g*), and that name occasionally appeared on his uniform or car.

Sterling, with the *g*, was also used, however, and curious media people eventually asked Marlin which was correct.

Finally, Marlin said it really didn't matter to him. "Just use what you want to," he said.

That didn't sit well with Marlin's mother, Eula Faye Marlin, however. She put out the word, in no uncertain terms, that Marlin's name was *Sterling* on his birth certificate, and that was what it would remain.

Any ideas that *Sterlin* might sound a little hipper or look a little cooler suddenly disappeared. Mama had spoken.

That's My Cap, Dude

Although he was born in Miami, Florida, Bobby Allison made Hueytown, Alabama, his racing home and became one of the state's most popular sports heroes.

He and his brother, Donnie, and Bobby's sons, Davey and Clifford, were particularly popular at Talladega Superspeedway, their "home" track.

Bobby won four times at NASCAR's biggest track. Following one of those wins, a fan got a little too up-close-and-personal with Allison.

After celebrating his win in victory lane, Allison jumped into a police car and rode to the grandstand gate to walk to the press box for the winner's interview. A huge crowd of fans had gathered at the gate in anticipation of Allison's arrival, and, as he walked through, a large male fan reached over and snatched Allison's cap.

Allison, who had remarkably quick reflexes, immediately grabbed the fan's arm and made him return the cap and apologize.

Allison enjoyed being part of the Alabama Gang, the collective nickname given to the Allisons and other top drivers from the state, but manners counted, too.

A Burning Desire

Lowe's Motor Speedway's prerace shows are legendary. Originally designed as a way to encourage fans to arrive at the track early on race day to spread out incoming traffic, the shows have become attractions in their own right. Motorcycles jump over school buses. School buses jump over motorcycles. Buildings explode. Military units invade the front stretch. Circus animals perform.

The shows require a lot of planning and preparation. And still there can be problems.

One show starred motorcycle stuntman Dennis Pinto. His specialty was riding a motorcycle into a parked car at 60 mph, flying through the air over the car, and landing in a bunch of cardboard boxes.

"A particularly cool stunt, but how can we take it to the next level?" asked Eddie Gossage, at that point the track's public-relations director. "Well, we thought that he could run into a big van and be much higher in the air. Then it hit one of us. What makes any stunt better? Fire. Add the element of fire.

"He was all for it. So we set him on fire. He takes off and hits the van. The van explodes. He flies through the air and lands in the boxes. The boxes were about eight feet tall.

"He didn't quite clear the bike, and his shins hit the handlebars and gashed both of them. Both of his shoes went flying and landed in the grandstands. But he still landed—on fire—in the boxes. What did we forget? He was on fire in cardboard boxes. He's buried inside there, and flames are everywhere. Firemen were trying to get extinguishers in there over the stacks of boxes. We finally got him out."

A Very Fast Police Officer

NASCAR driver Carl Edwards has some experience with law enforcement—literally.

Edwards has worked as a volunteer with the Boone County (Missouri) Sheriff's Department Reserve Division in the off-season and has participated in drug busts and traffic stops.

"He definitely has a talent for being a police officer," said Trevor Fowler, a department deputy. "He has common sense, and he's real smart."

Edwards participated in the bust of a meth lab after the sheriff's office got a tip that a teenage girl was being held against her will at her house.

Carl Edwards, here sitting in his car during practice for the NASCAR Sprint Cup Series Lenox Industrial Tools 301 at New Hampshire Motor Speedway on June 28, 2008, sometimes volunteers with the Boone County Sheriff's Department in the off-season.

"We got the call out to a rural area," Fowler said. "We went up to the door. Carl said he smelled something funny. We went around the corner of the house, and there was an ammonia smell. We snooped around a little and found a full-blown meth lab. The back door was ajar a little. We were expecting the worst but went in and arrested two people. It turned out the girl was part of the manufacturing process."

Fowler said Edwards' favorite part of the job—perhaps understandably—is responding to alarms with lights flashing, sirens wailing, and accelerator popping.

"He just dug that," Fowler said. "He liked that action. There was a lot of traffic."

According to Edwards, his work with the sheriff's department in his hometown of Columbia, Missouri, "has taught me a little about society, and I've gained a lot of respect for police officers. It all makes you understand there are a lot of things going on in the world, and a lot of them aren't good."

Executioner's Song

For a part-time NASCAR driver, road-race expert Boris Said built up a large fan base. The "Saidheads" could be seen at every track, many wearing the Afro-type wigs that duplicated Said's unusual hairstyle.

One of the tour's wackier drivers, Said has been known to create fun in just about every situation. He sort of startled himself on a prerace trip in 2003.

Said toured San Quentin Prison prior to the Cup Series race at Infineon Raceway in Sonoma, California. He went beyond the standard visitor's tour, however.

"I was in the execution chamber and laid down on the lethal-injection table," Said said. "The guard told me I was the first person to get up from that table. That was spooky."

In Search of Snakes

Phoenix International Raceway is one of the more interesting stops on the NASCAR circuit, in part because of its location. Plopped down into the Arizona desert, the track is surrounded by sandhills and cacti.

The area also has its share of snakes, including rattlers. Rattlesnakes have been found in the speedway's infield, which makes drivers and crew members a little more alert than normal when they visit.

Driver Carl Edwards took the opposite approach when he raced at the track in 2005. He and Tom Giacchi, his motor-coach driver, wandered into the hills adjacent to the track with the specific goal of finding snakes or scorpions.

"I grew up in Missouri," Edwards said. "We don't get to see stuff like that. We have deer. Deer are cool, but scorpions are pretty intriguing."

Edwards and Giacchi didn't root out any snakes, but they located one scorpion.

Take Jeff Out of the Ballgame

Jeff Gordon is one of NASCAR's most polished and poised drivers. He knows what to say and when to say it, and his on-screen presence has earned him a hosting spot on *Saturday Night Live* and frequent appearances on *Live with Regis and Kelly*.

So it came as something of a surprise in 2005 when Gordon was a special guest at the Chicago Cubs' Wrigley Field, and he botched his moment in the sun.

Prominent Wrigley visitors are frequently asked to lead the crowd in the singing of "Take Me Out to the Ball Game" during the seventh-inning stretch, and Gordon was picked for that honor. His rendition of the song wasn't exactly a landmark moment in music, and he sent a disturbing murmur through the crowd—plus caused some boos—at one of baseball's most cherished ballparks when he mistakenly called it "Wrigley Stadium."

Gordon suffered unmerciful kidding about his Chicago performance in the NASCAR garage area. "It's definitely a moment I'm not proud of," he said later.

Not Exactly the Daytona 500

When is a 500-mile race not a 500-mile race? When there's an energy crisis.

Motorsports series in the United States were dealt a blow in 1974 when a severe gasoline shortage caused long lines at service stations and some targeted auto racing as a waste of fuel.

NASCAR president Bill France Jr. was ready to counter talk of curtailing auto racing to save fuel. He introduced results of a study that showed that more fuel was used to fly professional football teams from one city to another than was used by all the cars in a single NASCAR race.

Very aware of the potential public-relations problem he faced, however, France made a concession to the situation. He cut the Daytona 500 by 50 miles (although the *Daytona 500* name didn't change).

The fuel crisis soon eased, and so did the threats to auto racing.

It's All in a Name

NASCAR fans have been known to do rather outlandish things. Some get married in a speedway victory lane. Others decorate their bodies with driver-specific tattoos. Some spend thousands of dollars to turn their dens into rooms celebrating their favorite drivers.

Few, though, have gone as far as Gwendetta Jamison of Roanoke, Virginia.

When Jamison gave birth to twins on January 1, 2003, she named one child Sterling and the other Marlin after NASCAR driver Sterling Marlin.

Marlin had the heavier foot. He weighed 6 pounds, 2 ounces. Sterling weighed 5 pounds, 13 ounces.

Fix That Hearse—Slowly

Longtime NASCAR driver Ted Musgrave, who has enjoyed much success in the Craftsman Truck Series, relaxes off the track by restoring old vehicles.

Cars from the 1950s are particularly attractive to Musgrave. He has restored 1958 Buicks and Fords and a 1956 Thunderbird, in addition to a variety of hot rods and street rods.

Also from the '50s is Musgrave's most unique old vehicle—a 1953 Cadillac hearse.

For any number of reasons, Musgrave has restored that one slowly.

Beer for Everybody!

The Miller Brewing Co. came up with a great idea to promote its product—and its driver, Rusty Wallace—prior to the 2003 Daytona 500.

The company announced before the race that it would give a six-pack of Miller Lite beer to every fan (of drinking age) at the track if Wallace won the 500.

Miller was pretty safe making that offer. Wallace had never won the 500 and, in fact, retired from driving without winning it.

Still, it was a unique promotion that earned the beer and the driver a ton of publicity.

"All the other beer companies went nuts because they didn't dream up the idea first," said Wallace, who had a longtime sponsor relationship with Miller. "It has been on every radio and TV station. It was even on *The Tonight Show*. That was pretty cool. I've got to hand it to them. They finally got balls to get out there and get it done instead of a conservative approach. They're rocking, man."

Wallace said the chance to win a six-pack encouraged fans of other drivers to pull for him, too.

Armistice Signs

The history of NASCAR racing is full of unusual names.

Some of the most memorable have been nicknames—the King (Richard Petty), the Silver Fox (David Pearson), the Intimidator (Dale Earnhardt Sr.)—but a few real names have attracted attention, too.

What other sport has had such monikers as Crawfish Crider, Gober Sosebee, Runt Harris, Speedy Thompson, Fireball Roberts, Cotton Owens, and Banjo Matthews?

Then there is the case of Ken Marriott, a Baltimore driver who raced in five Cup races from 1949 to 1959. He won the NASCAR Modified championship in 1957 and earned a sort of asterisk by his name by finishing last in the inaugural Daytona 500 in 1959. That was his last Cup race.

What's so unusual about Marriott's name? He was born November 11, 1919, exactly a year after the armistice ending World War I was signed. So his parents named him Ken Armistice Marriott.

Marriott died in 1998 in Clearwater, Florida.

A Doctorate in Stock Cars

The academic world and NASCAR? Yes, there is the occasional intersection between the two.

A major one occurred during the 2002 season when James Todd, a 31-year-old doctoral candidate at the University of California at Santa Cruz, lived a racing fan's dream. As part of a research project for his doctorate, Todd rode along for the entire NASCAR Cup schedule in a 1987 motor home working on a paper he called *Southern Culture and Stock Car Racing.*

Of primary interest to Todd were the Southern origins of NASCAR-style racing, how that Southern flavor is perceived as the circuit tours the country, and how NASCAR's marketing machinery has evolved over the years.

Over the season's 10-month span, Todd interacted with and interviewed fans, drivers, crew members, team owners, NASCAR officials, and news-media representatives. He tried to get "the big view" of the sport from all angles, from the corporate boardrooms to the infield barbecues.

"I have participated in a variety of parties," he said from his infield base. "I've been offered moonshine. It was my first time for that. Redneck horseshoes is one of the biggest things I've learned. You take toilet seats and throw them around large orange cones. I loved it.

"NASCAR has a very rich heritage over 50 years, so this is about trying to think about the history of region-making and also what happens when it goes to different places. How are regions made? What's the tension between a product, supposedly marked as Southern, when it goes to other places? How does culture travel?"

A Footrace in the Wrong Place

NASCAR racetracks aren't exactly the open highway, but you might not know that from the occasional visitors who show up to travel them.

Deer, rabbits, woodchucks, and dogs—just to name a few—have been spotted on speedway courses during races over the years.

The strangest visitor, though? A race fan.

During a 1993 race at Pocono Raceway, Kyle Petty rolled out of the speedway's second turn and looked up to see a fan dashing across the track and running into the nearby woods.

"I think that's the most bizarre thing anybody can have happen," Petty said. "I can't imagine anything any more bizarre than to come out of a corner, look down the straightaway, and see somebody standing in the middle of the racetrack. That's probably the strangest thing, to me personally, I've ever been involved in, in any race."

The interloper was apprehended by authorities.

chapter 13

Wins, Records, and Speed

Joe Gibbs stands in the garage during practice for the Daytona 500 on February 16, 2008. As former coach of the Redskins and a NASCAR team owner, Gibbs can claim the unusual and impressive feat of leading winning teams in both the Daytona 500 and the Super Bowl.

Richard Petty and Dale Earnhardt won seven Cup championships, establishing a NASCAR record that other drivers eye with envy. Only a few will have the chance to shoot at that number.

There are other notable accomplishments, though. Joe Gibbs won both the Super Bowl and the Daytona 500, for example. That's unlikely to be duplicated. And there are special moments—for example, when Bobby Allison outraced his son, Davey, to win the Daytona 500 on a day that, sadly, he no longer remembers.

In a sport built on speed, the rush toward the front continues.

It's a Long Way to No. 7

Jeff Gordon surpassed Dale Earnhardt's 76 Cup victories in the 2007 season, but every driver continues to chase one of Earnhardt's greatest records, one he shares with all-time Cup-victory leader Richard Petty.

Petty won seven Cup championships—in 1964, '67, '71, '72, '74, '75, and '79. Earnhardt tied Petty's total by winning the title in 1994. It was Earnhardt's fourth championship in five years.

Earnhardt clinched his seventh title on October 23, 1994, by winning the AC-Delco 500 at North Carolina Motor Speedway, a track no longer on the Cup schedule. On that day, he talked a lot about the people who had helped him along the way—Ned Jarrett, Humpy Wheeler, Tiny Lund, and others—and paid tribute to Petty, who had retired as a driver two years earlier.

"It's going to take a long time to sink in before you've really got a grasp on seven championships," Earnhardt said. "I just tried to put it out of my mind on tying Richard Petty's record. I knew what it would mean. It would mean a lot to me, and I'm really proud and honored to be in the same group with him as far as being tied with him. He's still the King. He's done it all. He pioneered it and got us where we are today."

Earnhardt, who was killed in a crash at Daytona International Speedway in 2001, never wore the crown of champion again.

Gibbs: King of Two Sports

Few people in the world of professional sports will ever enjoy the depth and breadth of success that Joe Gibbs has achieved.

Teams led by Gibbs have won Super Bowls, NASCAR national championships, and the Daytona 500. To do two wildly diverse things so well has earned Gibbs, who tends to reject praise and spin it off on others, an unusual amount of attention from all sides of the sports landscape.

Gibbs, who has been a team owner in NASCAR since 1992, offers the opinion that auto racing and the National Football League, where he recorded top-of-the-game success with the Washington Redskins, aren't as different as they seem.

"I tell everybody it's amazing how close they are," Gibbs said. "It's all a people business. You don't win races with cars. You don't win in football with Xs and Os or with how smart you are. You win with people.

"You have owners in football; you have owners over here. You have quarterbacks over there; you have drivers over here. Coaches in football and crew chiefs in racing. The overriding thing on all of it is the people part, getting the right group of people together, sacrificing to the team, and putting aside your own goals."

When the success comes, Gibbs said, the real enjoyment comes in being able to share it with those people. He has won Cup championships with drivers Tony Stewart and Bobby Labonte and has seen the thrill associated with that accomplishment run through the extended families.

"Seeing them get the excitement and the joy—if it's Bobby Labonte, it's seeing his dad, Bob, and the family, Tyler and Madison [Labonte's children] and Donna [Labonte's wife]—that get to go with him in living out a dream," Gibbs said. "And then, all the people here, getting to experience that championship. Then a whole different set of characters with Tony and all the people around him and Zippy [crew chief Greg Zipadelli] and his family.

"You get a big kick out of that, because they staked their careers and came with you and said, 'This is where we want to race.'"

Drivers Adjusted to Speed Jumps

Ned Jarrett, twice a NASCAR Cup champion (in 1961 and 1965), experienced both the pioneer days of racing and its move toward bigger, faster speedways. He retired in 1966, even as his career was purring along nicely.

Jarrett raced in the bumping and banging days of the half-mile dirt tracks and as the sport accelerated onto the much faster surfaces of tracks like Daytona International Speedway, which was a world away from tiny bullrings. Daytona opened in 1959.

Although speeds jumped by multiples, most drivers seemed to take the changes in stride. "The speeds were much higher than we had run before, and certainly there was concern about the extra danger that would be involved with the increased speeds," Jarrett said. "There probably were a lot of drivers who were very concerned about it, but speeds are normally relative to conditions. I think that's the way most of them looked at it.

"It never felt like you were running that fast. Daytona was bigger and wider than anything we had run on, so it just didn't feel like you were running that fast. It was sort of like going down the interstate at 75 miles per hour. It doesn't feel like you're going that fast, but you get on a two-lane road out in the country and go 75, and it feels like you're literally flying."

Jarrett Didn't Bring the Silver Spoon

Family connections are visible throughout NASCAR racing, and some drivers would have had a difficult time connecting with good rides if their fathers and brothers had not paved the way for them.

Still, being the son or brother of a great driver isn't all peaches and cream. Imagine following such greats as Richard Petty, David Pearson, and Dale Earnhardt into the driver's seat. Fair or not, much is expected.

In some cases, perhaps, driving with that famous family name is a burden.

For Dale Jarrett, son of two-time NASCAR champion Ned Jarrett, that decidedly was not the case.

"If there's a burden attached to it, it's more of what other people look for than what I look for," he said. "I just expect the most out of myself. It's not because of what Dad did or anything.

"I'm very competitive, and I want to win, not because Ned Jarrett was a champion, but because of what Dale Jarrett wants to do."

Too often, the thinking is that close relatives of drivers get the silver-spoon treatment, that they're handed the keys to everything along the way. Not true in his case, Jarrett said.

"He's been able to open some doors for me, although he hasn't just handed things to me, and I've appreciated that," Jarrett said. "He's really helped me to learn the business end of the sport and warned me how tough it was going to be."

Jarrett drove to the 1999 NASCAR Cup championship, joining his father at the top level of the sport.

A Special Victory for Martin

Sometimes the race victories are important because of the race status—the Daytona 500, the Coca-Cola 600, the Brickyard 400. On other occasions, it's the money. Occasionally, it's the pride associated with winning at a driver's "home" track.

On August 22, 1998, however, none of the statistics or the size of the paycheck or almost anything else meant much to Mark Martin. He had won the Goody's 500 at Bristol Motor Speedway, and the emotion attached to the victory was almost more than he could handle.

On August 8 of that year, Martin's father, Julian; his step-mother, Shelley; and his half-sister, Sarah, were killed in the crash of a private airplane. The next race was at Michigan International Speedway, and a grieving Martin hoped to win in memory of his family members. He had to wait until Bristol.

"I cried last week because I didn't get to dedicate a win to my dad and Shelley and Sarah," Martin said, awash in the emotions of the win. "This was for them. He would have been proud of this one tonight.

"You know, my relationship with my dad goes way beyond father and son. My dad was fun, and I will miss having fun with him.

That's what I hate the most is that he was great with Matt [Martin's son], and I'll miss that, but now it's time to move on. We've been through it, we've been to the depths, and now we're coming out of it and moving on."

NASCAR Invades the White House

It was a sight one doesn't often see from the steps of the White House: four NASCAR stock cars lined up on the driveway, with a White House fountain bubbling and the Washington Monument resplendent in the distance.

This was September 1978, and it was the fulfillment of a campaign promise president Jimmy Carter had made to the NASCAR community. "If I'm elected president," Carter, a NASCAR fan, had said, "I'll have you guys up to the White House."

As fulfillment of a campaign promise, Jimmy and Rosalyn Carter held a NASCAR dinner at the White House in September 1978, though President Carter could not attend due to Mideast peace talks. Pictured here are, left to right, Cale Yarborough, Rosalyn Carter, David Pearson, Benny Parsons, and Bud Moore.

The NASCAR dinner—there was roast beef, ham, potato salad, cornbread, and strawberry shortcake—took place on the South Lawn, and entertainment was provided by country-western singer Willie Nelson, another favorite of Carter's. A good time was had by all, except, ironically, the president, who missed the event because he was involved in Mideast peace negotiations at nearby Camp David.

First Lady Rosalynn Carter served as the hostess.

The president's wife started the party by waving a green flag, and drivers David Pearson and Cale Yarborough, crew chief Jake Elder in Benny Parsons' Chevrolet, and team owner Bud Moore in Bobby Allison's Ford drove their cars slowly around the circular driveway.

Hundreds of NASCAR drivers, team owners, officials (including NASCAR president Bill France Jr. and his father, Bill Sr.), and other racing people attended the dinner. Several toured the White House.

The partygoers danced the night away to Nelson's music, led by the president's brother, Billy, who told reporters he didn't go to the White House often but wouldn't miss the visit by NASCAR folks.

NASCAR Meets Le Mans

The 24 Hours of Le Mans and NASCAR racing are separated by an ocean and an idea—Le Mans is about exotic sports cars, while NASCAR is about stock cars, but the two came together for a brief flirtation in the 1970s.

A promotional idea hatched by NASCAR president Bill France resulted in some NASCAR-type stockers racing against the prototype sports cars at Le Mans in 1976. France called the cars Grand Internationals. They were basic Cup-series race cars with modifications to make them run better on the French road course.

They had no chance of beating the smaller, faster sports cars, but the hulking American stockers were a big hit. Their size and the thundering noise they produced enthralled the French crowd, and newspapers quickly labeled the Grand International car "Le Monster."

Cup drivers Dick Brooks and Dick Hutcherson drove the cars, which were owned by longtime NASCAR team owner Junie Donlavey.

"How the crowd reacted was unbelievable," Donlavey remembered. "Dick [Brooks] came in from a practice and left the car. I got in it to move it. People converged around it, and they kept coming, just crowding around. They were front, rear, hanging all over it. I couldn't see a thing. The people over there really took to it good."

France Touched His Hometown

When Bill France Jr. died in 2007, his accomplishments as top gun at NASCAR and International Speedway Corporation were celebrated. Less was known of his private life as a resident of Daytona Beach, Florida, where NASCAR is headquartered.

France fought numerous illnesses over the final years of his life. Few people knew all the details, but it was clear, even as he struggled with health problems, that he remained the strong individual his coworkers and contemporaries had come to know.

Richie Tucker was one of those France befriended on the sideline. Tucker, 70 years old, owns a Daytona Beach shoe-repair shop. France began stopping in the shop in the 1960s and had his shoes shined once or twice a week.

When Hurricane Charley hit the Florida coast in the summer of 2004, Tucker's shop was flooded and its roof caved in. The next time France stopped in, he had a question for Tucker.

"He said, 'Richie, how's business? You operating in the green or the red?'" Tucker said. "I said, 'A little of both.' He stood up on the shoeshine stand and reached in his front pocket and counted out 10 $100 bills and handed them to me. He said, 'Is that enough?'"

Every Christmas, Tucker said, France stopped by his shop and gave him, his wife, and his brother $100 each.

"He was white, and I'm black, but he was just like a big brother to me," Tucker said. "That's how he treated me."

Tucker was one of 2,000 people at France's memorial service in Daytona Beach on June 7, 2007.

A Major Crossroads

November 15, 1992, is one of the landmark dates in NASCAR history.

The final race of the '92 season was held that day at Atlanta Motor Speedway, and the tides of history intersected in several notable ways in the suburbs of the South's biggest city.

Perhaps most importantly, the Hooters 500 was Richard Petty's last race as a driver. The final event of the sport's most successful racer and the man who was most responsible for popularizing NASCAR in its middle years drew much media attention.

Lost in Petty's big moment was the fact that the 500 also marked the Cup debut of another driver—a promising youngster from Indiana via California, a kid named Jeff Gordon.

Petty and Gordon shared the stage with the ending of a remarkable run for the Cup championship. When the final race got the green flag, Davey Allison, Alan Kulwicki, and Bill Elliott were in the running for the championship.

Allison had fought through injuries that season to remain in the hunt for the title and took the lead into the Atlanta race. Kulwicki, an invader from Wisconsin and an unlikely championship challenger because he was operating his own team with relatively tiny resources compared to most of the competition, was within striking distance, as was Elliott, the prototypical Southern racer and the series champion in 1988.

The day ended with Kulwicki, ever the tactician, playing the race perfectly, leading enough laps to edge Elliott for the championship after Allison crashed. Elliott won the race, and Kulwicki was second, but the crucial laps-led category gave Kulwicki the title.

Petty also crashed during the race, and Gordon, also involved in a wreck, started what would become a spectacular career with an unspectacular 31st-place finish.

Allison was crushed by the day's circumstances. He couldn't believe his search for a first Cup championship had ended with such sour luck and a third-place points finish, 63 behind Kulwicki.

"Why does my luck go this way?" he asked no one in particular.

Two of the men in that season-ending drama would be in the news again the next year, but for tragic reasons.

On April 1, 1993, Kulwicki, the reigning Cup champion, was killed in the crash of a private plane near Bristol, Tennessee.

As the sport mourned, Allison told friends he finally understood why he didn't win the 1992 championship. "That was Alan's last chance," he said.

Incredibly, only three months later, Allison was dead. He died July 13, 1993, from injuries suffered in a helicopter crash at Talladega Superspeedway in Alabama.

As NASCAR stopped to mourn once more, memories of that season-ending race in Atlanta returned to the forefront.

A Daytona 500 Lost to Memory

One of the biggest moments of Bobby Allison's racing career— perhaps what should be his brightest memory—is lost to him.

Because of life-threatening head injuries he suffered in the Pocono Raceway crash that ended his driving career, Allison doesn't remember significant parts of his racing life.

One of the days he desperately wants to remember is the February afternoon when he raced with and outran his son, Davey, to win the 1988 Daytona 500.

"In 1988 at age 50 I won the third 'Super Bowl' of my career with the best young man in racing second to me, but I still don't remember 1988," Allison said. "It's kind of tough in a way. Sitting here right now, it hurts, and it annoys me that I have no memory of that.

"I sat down with a tape a few months ago and put it in the machine and watched the entire race flag-to-flag to see if it would do anything for me. It looks like a movie somebody made somewhere that kind of looks like something that maybe I had done one day."

Ironically, the victory was the last of Bobby Allison's career. Four months later, his car was T-boned in a vicious crash at Pocono, and he never drove again.

In 1993 Davey Allison was killed in a helicopter crash at Talladega Superspeedway.

"Front Row Joe" for Sure

Veteran NASCAR driver Joe Nemechek earned the nickname "Front Row Joe" for his skill at qualifying. When he finally finished a race on the front row, winning a Cup event for the first time in September 1999 at Loudon, New Hampshire, the circumstances were more than a little unusual.

A month before scoring his first career win, Nemechek had been told by car owner Felix Sabates that the ride in the No. 42 Team Sabco car would not be Nemechek's the following season. The team had struggled, and Sabates was looking for a fresh approach for the new season.

Nemechek needed 180 race starts to win in the Cup Series.

Sabates, one of the Cup garage's most popular characters, missed Nemechek's win because he was attending a Carolina Panthers National Football League game in Charlotte, North Carolina.

He congratulated Front Row Joe by telephone.

Wisdom at a Country Store

Although driver Ricky Craven is well known in his native New England, he isn't necessarily a familiar face everywhere else. Or at least that's what he thought.

While driving to Martinsville Speedway for a race in 2002, Craven, taking some back roads, stopped for gas at an old service station in the country. He walked inside and met three old men who were sitting in the station drinking coffee, chewing tobacco, and solving the world's problems.

Craven asked for directions to Martinsville. One of the men asked if he was going to the race, and he nodded. That sparked a 15-minute talk about some of the early races at the old half-mile track.

"It was priceless," Craven said, "the kind of thing you'd like to have on tape. They were talking about the races all the way back to the early 1950s."

Craven scored his first Cup victory at Martinsville in 2001, and he asked one of the men if he knew which driver had won that race.

"He spit out some tobacco," Craven said. "He paused for a long time, probably 10 seconds. I thought he hadn't heard me, and I was getting ready to walk out. Then, without even looking up, he said, 'You did.'"

First Win Brings Tears for Baker

Few things in NASCAR racing are as exciting as a driver's first victory.

Some score it relatively early in their careers; others struggle for season after season before finally riding into victory lane. Although many drivers go on to register numerous wins, they often choose that first victory as the most special of their careers.

For Buddy Baker, who won 19 Cup races in a career that stretched from 1959 to 1992, that first win came at his "home" track—Lowe's Motor Speedway (then Charlotte Motor Speedway)—in October 1967. It was such a joyous occasion that Baker could barely contain himself.

He cried in victory lane and wasn't ashamed of it.

"It's hard to explain that feeling between being just a driver and then being a winner on a big stage," Baker said. "You don't know whether to show your emotions or try to hold them back and look like everybody else that ever won a big race. But that first one—if you don't let it out, I think you would explode.

"Nothing will ever compare to your first major win. Since that is what I was going to do the rest of my life, it was really big."

The win gained additional sparkle because Buddy's father, Buck, a two-time Cup champion and a NASCAR pioneer, was there.

"My father had just had an accident, had a broken right leg, and was in a cast," Baker said. "I'm sure it was uncomfortable, and he took the time to make the trip from down in the pits all the way to the winner's circle. Then to see him, a grown man, one of the toughest guys in the sport, start to cry. If that doesn't get you, you can't be got.

"Up to that point, I felt like the little boy that needed somebody to tell him, 'It's going to be okay. You can do this.' That acceptance is something that every man looks at when they look at their dad. And [him] being a two-time Grand National champion, to me that was as important as the trophy or the win itself. It was like acceptance from my childhood hero.

"Then, to look out in the crowd and see people you went to school with and people you played football with, and my sister, who was killed in an auto wreck later in her life—just to look out and see your family members, it's a thing that can't be put in words."

On the Road with Junior

When Dale Earnhardt Jr. schedules a road trip with his friends, they should prepare for the unexpected. Since Junior rarely has more than one or two days off in a row, he makes full use of extended vacations.

In December 2001 Earnhardt Jr. and several of his friends drove from North Carolina to Buffalo, New York, to help another friend move. The trip was anything but ordinary.

"We got just past Greensboro [North Carolina] and turned off the interstate and just followed the compass from there on out," Earnhardt Jr. said. "We never got on another four-lane road. We went to Washington, D.C., and took our picture in front of the White House and in front of several of the monuments. We went through Gettysburg, Pennsylvania, and saw the battlefield, but it was two AM, so we couldn't see much."

Not surprisingly, the trip also involved a stopover at an off-the-beaten-path bar in Ohio. When word got out that Earnhardt Jr. was inside, the crowd grew from about 30 to roughly 300.

Martin Takes the Happy Road

Mark Martin, a racer's racer and one of the most respected drivers in the history of NASCAR, decided to trim his schedule in 2007 to more fully enjoy the final years of his career.

Some of Martin's friends were convinced that he couldn't do it, that he couldn't pull away—even for a week—from a sport to which he had been so dedicated. Martin's competition style defines intense. It was said that winning for him was more relief than joy.

Those closest to Martin, however, saw a distinct change in him after he announced his decision to go with an abbreviated schedule. He was obviously and outwardly happy, and, for a driver who had been labeled the eternal pessimist, that was unusual.

"He is having more fun than he has ever had in his life," said Jeff Burton, Martin's close friend and a former teammate. "He is honestly happier than I have ever seen him. He calls me and sounds like a teenage schoolgirl.

After Mark Martin decided to reduce his number of races and adopt a more abbreviated schedule, many people closest to him noticed that he became much more outwardly happy.

"It is kind of sickening, you know, to be honest. He is happier than I have ever seen him. He is in a better mood than I have ever seen him [in]. He is really relaxed, and he is very calm."

Even in victory lane, Martin was always thinking ahead to the next race, to the next date on the calendar. And, never predictable, Martin decided to give full-time racing another shot in 2009.

"You don't understand—when this race is over, it is over for everybody that is watching it, but it is not over for us," Burton said. "All it does is start a new week of worry about what is going to happen or what just happened. When you do that for a long period of time, it is a grind."

chapter 14

The Constant Is Change

Harry Gant, one of the most popular drivers in NASCAR history, did not become a full-time driver in his youth, as many do. Instead, he did not become a full-time Cup driver until he was 39 years old.

The only substantially consistent thing about NASCAR is change.

Rules change. Cars change. Drivers change. Even the schedule changes.

The racing of the 21st century bears little resemblance to the racing of the 1980s, much less the 1950s.

The future? The one thing for certain is that we'll see more changes.

Hey, Somebody Has to Lose

In the mid-1970s, NASCAR launched an effort to do away with so-called "deal" money—which some tracks paid to key drivers to be sure they would show up for their events—by designing a series of pay plans that benefited teams that agreed to run the full schedule of races.

Under such a system—one that is still in place today—track promoters can be reasonably certain that all top drivers will be on hand for their races and to promote the events accordingly.

In addition to boosting paychecks for leading teams, these payout plans also give more money to drivers and owners who typically run in the back of the pack, with little hope of victory.

This has caused a few complaints from top teams, which have taken the stance that more money should be placed in the higher-finishing race positions to encourage competition. Longtime team owner Bud Moore is among those who complained to NASCAR founder Bill France Sr., Moore's close friend, about the situation.

France didn't want to hear it.

"France told me, 'Hell, Bud, ya'll's asses have got to have someone to beat!'" Moore said.

The Air Blows In a New Day

NASCAR went through a difficult transition in the 1990s as aerodynamics became a much more important element in the performance of race cars.

For much of NASCAR history, the handling of a car, or how well it could be driven around a particular track, was determined mainly by adjustments made to the chassis underneath the car. As the shape of the cars' bodies became more important, emphasis shifted to learning how to make the cars glide through the wind better. It was a sea change for many, and it contributed to success for younger drivers who didn't grow up during the "under-the-car" era. As they arrived at the top levels of stock-car racing, they knew only about the aerodynamic factor. And they knew they had to be aggressively fast from the start.

"The shocks are so different," said Jeff Gordon. "The aerodynamics are so much different. The tires are different. What that does is force you to be extremely aggressive. What that means is the guys who are more aggressive are usually the ones who are going to benefit the most.

"Obviously, the young guys who haven't hit as many walls or lost control of their cars as often as some of the older guys have a lot more aggressiveness to put into that car. They also have come into it when the cars are like this."

Some older drivers found it difficult to adjust to the new world. But some were right at home.

"One of the things that impressed me the most about Dale Earnhardt [Sr.] was that he went through so many transitions of cars and downforce and tires and horsepower, and yet he was always able to come back and be competitive," Gordon said. "Rusty [Wallace] is another one of those guys. Bill Elliott is one of those guys. But it is tough, and it takes time to transition through it.

"Now we're getting closer and closer to being like Indy cars, where we have a lot of downforce and grip, and the speed doesn't drop off very much throughout the run. So the way you set the car up and the way you drive the car are completely different than the way it used to be."

Say, Don't I Know You?

If you can't necessarily drive like Dale Earnhardt Jr., looking like him might be the next-best thing.

That's how Chad McCumbee got a boost for his racing career.

A racer and a driving instructor at a high-performance driving school in North Carolina, McCumbee picked up a semi-starring role—and some valuable exposure—in the Dale Earnhardt Sr. movie 3 quite by accident.

Barry Pepper, who starred in the movie in the Earnhardt Sr. role, drove some laps at the racing school to become familiar with race cars and the racing environment. He met McCumbee and commented on how much the 20-year-old driver looked like Earnhardt Jr. One thing led to another, and before he knew it, McCumbee had agreed to play Junior in the movie.

"We were auditioning actors all over the place, and it was difficult because we could find good actors, but they didn't look like him," said Lynn Raynor, one of the film's producers. "When Barry spotted him and said that he was a dead ringer for Dale and has the right kind of demeanor and so forth, we felt like we'd give it a try. We brought him in and gave him acting lessons with a coach to see if he could do the role. He did really well. So we made the leap of faith. He was a terrific asset and was wonderful in the movie."

McCumbee, who hopes to build a Cup career, said he was "reasonably comfortable" playing Junior. "If acting is what I wanted to do, I probably would have been extremely nervous going into an audition like that, but I'm just out having fun. For me, it was just a cool thing to do. I thought it might open some doors and make me a more marketable person for racing."

Gentlemen, Start Your Baby Strollers

So, do you have a five-year-old who appears to have the right stuff to be a championship race-car driver?

If so, waste no time. Get him or her in go-carts now. You might already be behind the curve.

John Bickford, Jeff Gordon's stepfather, started Gordon in carts at the age of five, steadily moved him along to bigger and faster vehicles and—pow!—Gordon became a NASCAR superstar.

That's not going to happen with every five-year-old whose parents have big dreams, of course, but it is true that it's almost impossible to start too early these days.

Gordon's successful career has made Bickford a sort of go-to guy for questions about kids and racing. Now Gordon's business manager, he's usually happy to help.

Bickford also keeps an eye out for prospects.

"In 2000 Ray Evernham and I drove down to Daytona [for Daytona 500 activities] and decided to go to the sprint-car races," Bickford said. "We show[ed] up at Volusia County Speedway [a short track near Daytona Beach], and there's Kasey Kahne getting ready to qualify. I point[ed] to him and said, 'Watch him drive this car.' And Kasey gets quick time. I said, 'Watch him. You'll be racing against him if you don't have him racing for you.'"

Kahne now drives for Evernham Motorsports on the Cup circuit.

Gant Starts Late but Still Shines

At the age of 39 some NASCAR drivers are already planning what they'll do when they retire. Harry Gant didn't quite follow that route. He was 39 when he became a full-time Cup racer.

Gant, who eventually became one of the most popular drivers in NASCAR history, worked in his family's home-construction business in North Carolina and had no background in racing. In 1964 he began going to races at Hickory Speedway near his home and soon began sharing driving duties in a Hobby car owned by a friend. One thing led to another, and Gant won the track championship in 1965. He moved up to Late Model Sportsman cars and soon began competing in regional races against tougher competition, where he quickly gained a reputation as one of the best short-track racers in the country.

In the late 1960s and through the 1970s, Gant raced in NASCAR's national Late Model Sportsman series, where he competed with—and often beat—such short-track stars as Jack Ingram, Butch Lindley, and Gene Glover. That circuit eventually became the NASCAR Busch Series.

Gant made his Cup debut in 1973, but he didn't become a series regular until 1979. He raced for the Series Rookie of the Year title that season but lost it to a future superstar named Dale Earnhardt Sr.

Gant retired in 1994, but not before becoming the oldest driver—at 50 years and 158 days—to win a Cup race. He recorded that achievement at Pocono Raceway in 1990.

A year later Gant won the first four Cup races held in September to tie a modern-era record for most consecutive wins. The streak earned him the nickname "Mr. September." If not for a late-race brake problem the next week at North Wilkesboro Speedway, he would have stretched the run to five.

Finally, at 54 years old, he drove the last mile and was on his way to Hall of Fame membership.

New School and Old School Ride Same Trail

Over the past two decades, NASCAR racing has seen a steady progression in the arena of car preparation. Engineers have become more and more important as teams seek that extra edge. Still, though, old-school racers, the descendants of the shade-tree mechanics who started the sport more than a half-century ago, are represented.

Crew chief Greg Zipadelli, who has won championships with Tony Stewart, likes to think of himself as a blend of both. The trick, he says, is to find a happy balance between long-held, tried-and-proven methods and engineering input.

"Some weekends it's more engineering, some it's more old school," he said. "I think it just depends on what you're looking for and the circumstances you're in at that time. Half the time the engineers are telling me the things that won't work, and I'll figure out the things that will. That saves you time.

"We're fairly engineering-based on projects. We give them projects or places where we want to go and things we want answers to. They bring them to you, and you decide whether you want to use them or not. It's not like they're sitting there telling you how to set up a race car. It's more looking ahead and trying to give us tools we can look at and learn."

Zipadelli described himself as "somewhat old school in that, that's how I grew up, but I'm fairly aggressive in wanting to learn and look at new things all the time."

And the engineers are there to provide avenues for that exploration. All major Cup teams now have virtual platoons of engineers examining all aspects of their car preparation.

Sabates Races to the Good Life

One of the most remarkable stories in the NASCAR garage is that of Felix Sabates, part owner of the Chip Ganassi Racing with Felix Sabates team.

Sabates, once a majority owner of the team, came to the United States from Cuba in 1959. He was "flat broke," as he put it, and looking for the opportunity that freedom in the United States promised.

He found it in more ways than one.

"My family was very well-to-do," Sabates said. "We lost everything because of [Cuban dictator Fidel] Castro. We went from the top to the bottom. When people tell me how bad they have it—hey, I've been there."

Before the dramatic changes in Cuba, Sabates lived a life of ease. "We had seven full-time servants, and a chauffeur drove me to school," he said. "I didn't even know what it was like to tie my own shoelaces until I was seven."

But the Cuban revolution hit many wealthy families hard, and the Sabates family soon found itself on the outside looking in. Sabates left for the U.S. when he was 16 years old.

"I came over with my six brothers and my sister and my mother, and I was the only one working while we were living in a two-bedroom house with one bathroom," he said. "I worked 80 hours a week just to buy groceries."

When he arrived in Miami, Florida, from Cuba, Sabates had $25 in cash and two boxes of Cuban cigars. He sold the cigars to get more money.

He worked in a restaurant kitchen as a dishwasher and in a hospital as an orderly and performed "every kind of mediocre and low-paying job there was," he said.

He eventually moved to North Carolina and got a job selling cars. That led to a sales job with Tops Sales, a distributor of electronic toys and games. That was Sabates' break. Five years after joining the company, he had saved enough money to buy it. He had hit the game industry at the right time, and soon money was flowing.

In 1989 Sabates jumped into NASCAR Cup team ownership and began a journey that has made him one of the most popular people in the garage.

Although he sold most of his team to Ganassi, Sabates continues to show up at races and hang with his friends in the garage. He continues to be one of them, although their histories and his cross only within the boundaries of the American dream.

Stewart, Zipadelli Make Perfect Team

Tony Stewart didn't exactly overachieve in his introduction to stock-car racing in the Busch Series.

A winner in open-wheel racing, Stewart chose to detour to NASCAR and signed on with team owner Joe Gibbs. Gibbs put Stewart in Busch cars, and he couldn't break into victory lane.

It was somewhat surprising, then, when Stewart stormed the Cup Series ranks in 1999 to win three races and finish fourth in series points.

A big chunk of the credit went to new crew chief Greg Zipadelli, a man Stewart had not met before they were paired together by Gibbs.

"There's probably been three or four crew chiefs that I have had a relationship with like I have with Greg," said Stewart, referring to his years in other forms of racing. "Larry Curry was one of them, also, and there were two guys I ran Midgets for that were the same way. It's all about chemistry. You sit here thinking that you can put a crew chief and driver together working for the same cause, and how could they not get along? Like I said, in 20 years I've known four guys that fit the bill.

"If it was legal to marry two people, I'd marry my fiancée, and I'd make sure Greg was tied in there somehow, so he couldn't get away, either.

"It's weird. It really surprised both of us. I wouldn't have known Greg Zipadelli if I had tripped over him, until the first day that I saw him. To come in and have the kind of relationship we've had has been great."

Stewart and Zipadelli proved the relationship solid by going on to win Cup championships and becoming one of the longest-lasting driver–crew chief combos in the sport before Stewart departed for a new team in 2009.

Johnson Lost a Young Friend

The stories of Junior Johnson's moonshining days, a period that ultimately landed him in federal prison for almost a year, have become almost legendary, and Johnson admits to a certain nostalgic fondness for that time when he roamed North Carolina backroads delivering illegal liquor.

However, the roads of Wilkes County hold another Johnson story, too, and it is of the dark side.

In April 1990 a single-car accident near Wilkesboro took the life of a young man named Brent Kauthen. Brent, whose mother lived in Michigan, spent summers with Johnson beginning at the age of eight, after they met at a race, and became like a member of the family. He traveled with Johnson's racing team to summer events and, after high school, moved to North Carolina and attended North Carolina State University.

"I thought as much of him as if he'd been my own," said Johnson, who now has two children. "I enjoyed all the years I had with him. It was a sad situation. He was just at the point in his life when he would be stepping out into the world."

Saving the Best for Last

Virtually every NASCAR Cup race is a marathon. From 600 miles at Lowe's Motor Speedway to 500 laps at Martinsville, this brand of racing is the opposite of a sprint. When you buckle up here, it's for the long run.

In most cases, however, the critical decisions and on-track moves that determine race winners are made in the last five laps, and that reality requires that drivers save themselves and their thinking processes for the closing miles. After a long day or night of racing, it's suddenly time to decide how big the payday is going to be.

Does the driver's attitude and approach change in those final laps?

"Yes, but you can't let it change to the point of doing silly stuff," said veteran driver Jeff Burton. "You have to keep in mind that whatever you do in the last five laps could erase everything you've done in all the other laps. You can't do something stupid and take away all you've done.

"At the same time, that's the time you win the race or lose the race. That's the time to take advantage of all the work you've done."

Although most drivers are naturally tired at the end of a long race, their competitive nature kicks in for the closing miles, Burton says.

"I think adrenaline gets going," he said. "As long as you can keep the adrenaline from taking over your brain, that's good. A lot of people in all sports get too pumped up, and if you get too pumped up, you can make a mistake. But you have to be more pumped up than you were earlier in the race. If you're not, you're losing."

Mom and Pop Say It's Okay

When Ray Evernham left Hendrick Motorsports in the fall of 1999 to start his own NASCAR team, it ended one of the sport's great partnerships.

As crew chief for driver Jeff Gordon, Evernham won three Cup championships and dozens of races and helped Gordon become one of the best racers in the country. Evernham and Gordon seemed to work as one, their attitudes and approaches to racing very much the same. They could practically finish each other's sentences.

No one thought the pairing would last forever, but it still was something of a shock when Evernham decided to take an offer from DaimlerChrysler to become the company's lead team-owner when it reentered Cup racing in 2001. That resulted in Evernham leaving Hendrick in September 1999.

By January 2001, Evernham was ready to go for his first season as a team owner, but he admitted there was a long road ahead before his organization would reach a competitive level.

One of the factors, Evernham said with a smile, was youth.

"The average of the 19 team [one of his teams] is like eighth grade," he said. "We've got some young guys over there. You know when you go to get your NASCAR licenses and everybody has to bring permission slips from Mom and Dad that you've got a young team."

Burton: Making Top 10 Difficult

What's tougher—moving from the back of the NASCAR pack to the middle, or climbing from the middle to the top?

Veteran driver Jeff Burton articulated the general view in the garage that struggling to get into the top 10 is much more difficult than racing for wins once you get there. Generally, the drivers racing from 20th on back are struggling with a variety of issues, including keeping their rides or auditioning for better ones and staying in the top 35 in points to qualify for guaranteed starting spots.

"It's a harder fight to come from 30th to 10th than it is from 10th to fifth because from 30th to 10th you have all the people pulling in different directions, believing they know how to do it," Burton said. "That's a harder fight than the one you face when you start doing better."

Jarrett Bridged Two Eras

Ned Jarrett raced in NASCAR's Cup Series from 1953 to 1966 and won two championships and 50 races along the way.

Jarrett also had a foot in two eras. As he was preparing to end his career, stock-car racing was moving away from "showroom" race cars and into vehicles built specifically for racing. After several tragic accidents, racing's safety landscape also was changing for the better.

"In the 1950s the cars were pretty stock with just the basic roll bars," Jarrett said. "There was one roll bar over the driver's head. In the early 1960s that began to change with additional roll bars and, ultimately, the roll cage.

"It was sometime in 1963, I guess, that we started building race cars from the ground up. Up until then, you were taking a car off the showroom floor basically and building a race car out of it. Before the '60s, we used the old bench seats. Then the bucket seats came along. I never used one of the molded seats like they have today."

Fuel cells were developed after several horrific accidents involving fire, including the 1964 wreck at Charlotte (now Lowe's) Motor Speedway that resulted in the death of Fireball Roberts. A strong inner lining for tires also was developed in 1964 to give drivers a much better chance of keeping control of their cars when tires blew.

Jarrett retired just as the sport was becoming much safer for its competitors. He was only 34 years old. Did he leave too early? "No, it was time," Jarrett said.

One Phone Call Changes It All

The phone call that changed David Pearson's life came while he was putting a new roof on a house.

It was the spring of 1961, and Pearson had planned to enter an old Chevrolet he owned in the World 600 in May at Charlotte Motor Speedway. That ride would have been questionable at best; instead, Pearson got a phone call about driving for team owner Ray Fox Sr. in the 600. He jumped at the chance.

Fox, who had a vacancy on his team, called Pearson, who had been dominating Carolinas short tracks, on the advice of numerous friends and associates. Pearson showed up in Charlotte, jumped in the Fox Pontiac, and ran hot laps immediately.

David Pearson poses after he won the second annual World 600 at Charlotte Motor Speedway in Concord, North Carolina, on May 28, 1961.

"David came in off the track, and I asked him if anything was wrong with the car," Fox said. "He said, 'Well, it went so fast I don't know. I've never driven a car that fast.'"

The rest of the Pearson-Fox story reads in storybook fashion. Pearson won the race, although he had to wrestle with a flat tire over the final two laps. Victories at Atlanta and Daytona Beach followed, and Pearson was on the way to a highly successful NASCAR Cup career that eventually produced 105 victories.

"He just had a natural instinct about what to do," Fox said.

Pearson had driven his own cars in 22 Cup events in 1960, but the chance to drive for a top builder like Fox gave him his big break.

An Impressive Debut

Brian Whitesell, a quiet, low-key guy who has filled a number of roles at Hendrick Motorsports, was in a very bright spotlight on October 3, 1999, at Martinsville Speedway in Virginia.

Whitesell had been picked to fill a very important position—crew chief for Hendrick Motorsports driver Jeff Gordon. The vacancy occurred when Ray Evernham, Gordon's crew chief since the driver's Cup arrival, accepted an offer to direct Dodge's return to Cup racing. Immediately, there arose questions about how well Gordon could perform without the man who had guided his first years in the sport.

The answer came quickly. Gordon won his first race without Evernham, and Whitesell was in charge of the show.

"I had no reservations about taking this job," Whitesell said. "I knew we could go out the first week and win the race. If I didn't believe that, I wouldn't have done it."

That's Smart, but Can It

It happens in a NASCAR race every month or so—a driver roars away from his pit after a hurried pit stop with the catch-can still attached to his car.

The catch-can is held by a crew member and is designed to catch overflow as fuel is put into the car. In the rush of the moment, however, the can sometimes becomes stuck in the opening and leaves the pit with the car—a violation that results in a second pit stop.

Morgan-McClure Motorsports once devised a way around the problem, but its method didn't meet with the approval of NASCAR officials.

Mark Prater, the team's catch-can man, developed a tearaway tether that connected the can to Prater, thus making it unlikely that the driver could leave with the can.

NASCAR liked the idea but ultimately vetoed it because it feared that the driver might roar away with the catch-can man still attached to the tether.

"I appreciate the ingenuity of the teams coming up with that," said series director John Darby, "but we're a little more comfortable without crew members actually being attached to the race car."

chapter 15

Getting There

Jeff Gordon ushered in an age of younger drivers and the dispensation of the myth that age equates with wisdom.

How does one become a
NASCAR Cup driver, anyway?

A lot of it is luck. The right person happens to
see you at the right neighborhood track on the
right night, and the right connection is made.
Some of it is family. If your dad or your brother is a
racer, you automatically have a better shot.

Still, though, there's the talent.
You need some of that.

Hey, Man, Need a Driver?

There are only 43 starting positions in each NASCAR Cup race, and there are literally thousands of drivers who think they could fill them.

And, as numerous Cup drivers will confirm, many of the wannabes out there on dusty three-eighths-of-a-mile ovals in the boondocks could do the job just as well as they can. But they can't get that shot if they don't find the opening to racing's top level, and that task can be daunting—in fact, it's frequently impossible.

Many of those who get the break have an "in." They have a relative on a Cup team; they have a link to an executive in racing; a brother-in-law is a race-team attorney. Still others are noticed at the short-track level by a key member of a Cup team, and word quickly passes along the grapevine that Driver X has the tools to win at higher levels. There are driving schools across the country that promise to groom young drivers for stardom.

And then there's the story of Roush Fenway Racing driver Carl Edwards, who decided to try to separate himself from other aspiring drivers with, of all things, a business card.

"My mission was to let potential owners know that I wanted to drive race cars," Edwards said. "It was kind of awkward to just walk up to people and tell them, 'Hey, I want to drive your car.' So I thought having a business card would kind of make it a little more natural. I had a lot of people make fun of me, but it worked out.

"I didn't really know what I was going to put on it. I finally came up with, 'If you're looking for a driver, you're looking for me,' with my name and address. On the back I had my whole résumé."

He printed 3,000 cards at a cost of $130.

Edwards got a ride in the Craftsman Truck Series in 2002, and impressive showings there put him in the Roush Fenway Racing pipeline. Now he's one of the best in Cup racing.

Along the way, Edwards' parents invested about half of their savings to buy a United States Auto Club Silver Crown car to give their son a chance to show what he could do in a fast-paced asphalt race. "It was a huge risk money-wise, and not everybody thought it was a great idea," Edwards said. "But I'm glad we did it. That's when things started working out. I started getting hired by other folks."

And the business card didn't hurt.

Junior: Work Faster, Boy

In October 2006 the Cup race at Talladega Superspeedway in Alabama had the sort of ending that many fans have come to expect at the 2.66-mile track. The lead changes hands frequently in close competition at Talladega, and it did so on the last lap of the UAW-Ford 500.

Brian Vickers, seeking his first career Cup victory, sparked mayhem in the race's final mile when he turned Jimmie Johnson into Dale Earnhardt Jr. as the trio fought for the lead. Johnson and Earnhardt Jr. spun out, leaving the win to Vickers.

Controversy was expected, and it erupted. Earnhardt Jr. fans had a field day criticizing Vickers.

A few days after the race, however, Vickers got an endorsement from a considerable source—former NASCAR driver and team owner Junior Johnson.

Vickers visited Johnson, who was known to race aggressively in his time on the track, at his home near the Brushy Mountains of North Carolina.

"What would you have done differently?" Vickers asked as they talked about the Talladega race.

"I told him, 'Hey, I would have wrecked them three laps earlier,'" Johnson said with a smile.

Lap After Lap in the Wilderness

Although Sprint Cup drivers make their reputations—and most of their money—racing on the No. 1 motorsports series in the country, many of them detour to some other form of racing during the season, largely for the recreation.

Drivers who started on dirt often return to the soil after reaching Sprint Cup, mostly because it's so much fun.

Clint Bowyer fits in that category. Called in from the plains of Kansas to drive for Richard Childress' NASCAR team, Bowyer learned the sport on Midwestern dirt bullrings, then won the 2002 NASCAR Weekly Series Midwest Regional championship. Childress saw Bowyer run well in an Automobile Racing Club of America event at Nashville, Tennessee, and gave him his shot at the big time.

Bowyer is thrilled to be racing at his sport's highest level, but he also still digs the dirt.

"My most enjoyable moments were back home racing at the local dirt tracks and going from one track to another, racing every night for a week and a half," Bowyer said. "Those are the good old days. Just racers out there racing. Not a bunch of fans around. Nobody knows or even cares [who] you are. I really enjoy those days. There were a lot of wild nights in dumpy motels across the country, sleeping 10 to 15 guys in a hotel room to get by."

The difference now, he says, is that performance is expected, not optional.

"Back then there wasn't any pressure," he said. "You'd go out and you'd race and have fun and have a beer afterward and go out and get up the next morning and get things rolling again for the next night. Now, you run bad, you've got a lot of people to answer to. You've got a pretty angry boss, you've got sponsors that are wondering what's going on, and that's your career. That's your life. That's how you put food on the table."

And a Child Shall Lead Them

The topic of age has been an interesting element in NASCAR racing in recent years.

Since the 1992 appearance of Jeff Gordon, who made it fashionable to hire younger drivers, Cup racing has changed dramatically. Gordon's success and his star appeal encouraged team owners to look closer at younger drivers when filling vacancies, and the idea that drivers needed years of Cup experience to be successful fell into disfavor.

In recent seasons, it has become unusual for drivers upward of 40 years old to win races. In the pre-Gordon era, advanced age meant wisdom and a better shot at winning.

Six of Dale Earnhardt Sr.'s seven Cup championships were scored after his 35th birthday. Two NASCAR Rookies of the Year were in their late 40s—Dick Trickle was 48 in 1989, and Jimmy Hensley was 47 in 1992.

"This all has a lot to do with Jeff Gordon coming along," Matt Kenseth said. "He started running good and winning right away and beating a lot of the older, experienced drivers. I think a lot of owners and sponsors looked to that and said if we get a young driver it makes a lot more sense, because we have a lot more time to work with him.

"It used to be that people were basically recycling guys over and over and over until they were in their fifties, and then they left. Now there are a lot of people who are getting opportunities who are 20 years old. The opportunities are much easier to come by."

It also doesn't hurt, Ricky Rudd said, that most sponsors prefer younger faces.

"The sponsors are out selling suntan oil," Rudd said. "They don't necessarily want a guy 45 years old in their commercials."

Casey Cashes In

Roger Mears shed more than a few tears as he watched his son, Casey, roll into victory lane for the first time in a NASCAR Cup race in the 2007 Coca-Cola 600 at Lowe's Motor Speedway.

It was a long time coming, and Roger knew more about the struggles than most. Roger ran Indy cars in the early 1980s.

Casey began his major-league racing career in CART Indy cars before detouring to NASCAR.

Casey started racing in Cup races in 2003 and bumped his way through four winless seasons before scoring with Hendrick Motorsports in '07.

"Casey has been outstanding, honestly, from day one in everything he's raced," Roger said. "I knew that he was really a talent and had a good head on his shoulders. I thought he would come over into the stock-car thing and do better than he has more quickly. It's not because of him. It's because the competition is stiffer than I thought it was.

"It takes a Rubik's Cube combination of so many things to be successful in NASCAR. In some other series, you can get the car close, and the driver can make it happen. Here, the cars are so close that the suspension being off just a tick can put you 35th instead of fifth.

"Casey is so tough mentally, though. He calms me down. Every few weeks or so, I'll get so frustrated that I'll start saying stuff I probably shouldn't say. He's oozing with confidence in himself. No matter how bad things look, he can fall back on that."

The Mears family retreats at the end of the season to a home Roger owns in Mexico for some rest and rehabilitation. The rest normally includes some serious dune-buggy riding.

A Step Back Equals a Leap Forward

It was clear early on that Kyle Busch had the special talents needed to be a race-car driver. He raced his older brother, Kurt, successfully in go-carts in the family's driveway.

Kyle succeeded at short tracks near his Las Vegas home as a teenager and, by the age of 16, had moved into a ride in NASCAR's Craftsman Truck Series, quite a leap for a kid still in high school.

There was the assumption that Busch would be in the Cup Series before his 18th birthday.

It was abundantly clear well before his 18th birthday that Kyle Busch had what it takes to be a top-notch race-car driver.

NASCAR threw a wet towel on those thoughts, however, by changing its rules and declaring that drivers younger than 18 could not race in any of its top three series.

Busch was a racer suddenly homeless. He dropped down to the American Speed Association Series in 2002 and tried to learn more through his disappointment.

Eventually, Busch moved on to Cup races, won, and became one of the series' top young drivers.

"I would have told you a couple of years ago that the 18-year-old thing was a stupid move," Busch said. "I felt like the whole world was taken from me, and what I wanted, I couldn't have anymore. For me, being that young, I thought, 'I'm done, there's no more of me.' You're there, and you get kicked out, and you think, 'Well, who's going to want me now?'

"As it's turned out, it was probably one of the best moves that's come about in my career. I certainly didn't realize it then. Going to ASA and learning the things I was able to learn there about longer races, pit stops, strategy, this and that, was really, really good for me, instead of just driving the race car and have the crew chief make all the calls. I kind of have a sense of what I need to know about a race and how it plays out.

"Being able to run those different series at that young of an age helped me out. Now if I was in the Cup Series at 18, I would be lost. Completely lost."

"Brave" Edwards Loses Shirt

Subscribers to *ESPN The Magazine* were greeted by an unusual cover when their copies of the February 27, 2006, issue arrived.

Staring at them from a racing shop with his fire suit opened to his waist, exposing his buff physique, was NASCAR driver Carl Edwards.

It was obvious from the photo that Edwards, one of several drivers devoted to staying in tip-top shape, spends hours in the gym.

Still, the fact that Edwards agreed to appear on the cover of a major national magazine in such an unusual pose stirred interest in the garage.

"I was at a newsstand, and I did come across that," said Jeff Gordon, who was asked about the photo. "The first thing I said was, 'Wow, he's brave.'"

Bombs Away, Boys

NASCAR drivers Jon Wood and Brian Vickers have been friends since childhood and crammed a lot of adventures into their formative years.

Like the time they built a few bombs in the Wood Brothers race shop in Stuart, Virginia.

Wood owned several radio-controlled airplanes—it's still a hobby of his—and he and Vickers packaged small explosive devices inside one of the fliers. They sent the plane aloft and used a remote-control trapdoor to drop the bombs in the big yard outside the shop.

It was entirely safe, or at least as safe as an activity could be when the Wood and Vickers youngsters were involved.

Early in their racing careers, they shared an apartment in Greensboro, North Carolina, and friends say they basically "used it up" before they departed for fresher climates.

"It's a wonder any of us survived it," said Eddie Wood, Jon's father.

Edwards Bounces Back

It would have been difficult for Carl Edwards' first full season in Cup racing—2005—to be better.

He won four races, finished third in the point standings, and became his sport's newest young star—all as a rookie, although he had run 13 races the previous season and thus didn't qualify technically as a rookie contender.

With that background, Edwards roared into 2006 expecting even bigger things. What he got was a big thud.

The season held no wins for the Roush Racing driver, and he was never able to advance higher than 12th in the point standings. It was a humbling situation for a young driver on the move.

"In '05 when the car was perfect and it handled really well, we were superfast," Edwards said. "And then in '06, for whatever reason, when the car was perfect and handled really well, we were usually running about third, so it was just a little bit different.

"The toughest thing for us was just the luck. The Poconos—both of those we had terrible luck, and at both Daytonas, just terrible luck. Right there is 350 points or something just in those four races, and the year before it seemed like some of those things would work out on the good side of that. That was really the tough part for me."

It wasn't entirely unexpected, though, Edwards said. He had been around enough racetracks to understand the ebb and flow.

"There are times when things go great, and you can't do anything wrong, and there are times when you just can't get anything right," he said. "I guess the biggest thing and the thing that really helped me the most about having that year is that it really made me look at what makes a race go good or bad and to realize the things I can do to control it and then how not to let it get you down because it is frustrating.

"The bottom line is you can only do what you can do. You can only focus on the things you can control, and that's it."

Edwards rebounded the next season to return to championship contention.

sources

In addition to the below-listed sources, certain material in the book came from press conferences and open media sessions.

Benyo, Richard. *Superspeedway: The Story of NASCAR Grand National Racing.* New York: Mason-Charter, 1977.

Dutton, Monte (ed.). *Taking Stock: Life in NASCAR's Fast Lane.* Dulles, VA: Brassey's, Inc., 2002.

Fielden, Greg. *Forty Years of Stock Car Racing Vol. I: The Beginning, 1949–1958.* Surfside Beach, SC: Galfield Press, 1988.

———. *Forty Years of Stock Car Racing Vol. II: The Superspeedway Boom, 1959–1964.* Surfside Beach, SC: Galfield Press, 1988.

———. *Forty Years of Stock Car Racing Vol. III: Big Bucks and Boycotts, 1965–1971.* Surfside Beach, SC: Galfield Press, 1989.

———. *Forty Years of Stock Car Racing Vol. IV: The Modern Era, 1972–1989.* Surfside Beach, SC: Galfield Press, 1990.

———. *Forty Years of Stock Car Racing: Forty Plus Four, 1990–1993.* Surfside Beach, SC: Galfield Press, 1994.

Golenbock, Peter, and Greg Fielden (editors). *The Stock Car Racing Encyclopedia.* New York: MacMillan, 1997.

Hembree, Mike. *NASCAR: The Definitive History of America's Sport.* New York: HarperEntertainment, 2000.

Jensen, Tom. *Cheating: An Inside Look at the Bad Things Good NASCAR Winston Cup Racers Do In Pursuit of Speed.* Phoenix: David Bull Publishing, 2002.

Tucker, Tom, and Jim Tiller. *Daytona: The Quest for Speed.* Daytona Beach, FL: The News-Journal, 1994.